Poetry in Motion

Surrey Vol II
Edited by Steve Twelvetree

 Young**Writers**

First published in Great Britain in 2004 by:
Young Writers
Remus House
Coltsfoot Drive
Peterborough
PE2 9JX
Telephone: 01733 890066
Website: www.youngwriters.co.uk

SB ISBN 1 84460 410 1

Foreword

This year, the Young Writers' 'Poetry In Motion' competition proudly presents a showcase of the best poetic talent selected from over 40,000 up-and-coming writers nationwide.

Young Writers was established in 1991 to promote the reading and writing of poetry within schools and to the youth of today. Our books nurture and inspire confidence in the ability of young writers and provide a snapshot of poems written in schools and at home by budding poets of the future.

The thought effort, imagination and hard work put into each poem impressed us all and the task of selecting poems was a difficult but nevertheless enjoyable experience.

We hope you are as pleased as we are with the final selection and that you and your family continue to be entertained with *Poetry In Motion Surrey Vol II* for many years to come.

Contents

St Bede's School, Redhill

Kathryn Pendrous (11)	48
William Payne (11)	48
Sarah Isherwood (13)	49
Hayley Miles (14)	50
Laura Shaw (13)	50
Patrick McKenna (11)	51
Roisin Skinner (11)	52
Melanie Failes (14)	53
Richard Miles (14)	54
Gareth Pettit (12)	55
Danny St John-Hall (13)	56
Jonathan Murphy (13)	57
Claudia Baxter (14)	58
Abbie Parsons (11)	59
Natalie Gill (13)	60
Constance Mandair (13)	61

Selsdon High School

Ryan Heartfield (13)	62
Lauren Cooke (15)	63

Sutton High School

Sameera Ali (12)	63
Melanie Ranaweera (14)	64
Lizzi Yentumi (11)	65
Niamh Connaughton (12)	66
Sophie Penwarden (11)	67
Carla Busso (12)	67
Harriet Trefusis (12)	68
Laura McLean	68
Emma Rice (14)	69
Alyce Hayes (12)	69
Saman Zaman & Helen Sumping (14)	70
Faizah Ahmed (12)	71
Sana Sheikh (12)	71
Grace Lavelli (12)	72
Lucy Parter (12)	73
Charlotte Howson (12)	73
Alice Kendle (13)	74

Esther Nicoll (13)	74
Natasha Ward (13)	75
Barira Gore (16)	75
Catherine Langley (12)	76
Catherine Kilkenny (12)	77
Mina Ghosh (11)	78
Emma Harkins (12)	79
Kyndra Vorster (11)	80
Antonia Williams (14)	80
Krupa Thakker (11)	81
Hannah Nicoll (13)	81
Jennifer Ferguson (11)	82
Helen Thorpe (14)	83
Nivedita Chakrabarti (13)	84
Sophia Kavanagh (11)	85
Lucy Bidmade (15)	86
Shaline Fazal (12)	86
Alice Heathfield (11)	87
Charlotte Irvine (11)	88
Sarah Daoud (11)	89
In-Young Choi (13)	90
Nancy Godden (12)	91
Laura Hamer (12)	92
Hayoon Lee (12)	93
Zara Syed (13)	94
Sabrina Marsh (12)	94
Alina Fazal (15)	95
Emma McLean (14)	96
Katie Madden (15)	97
Se-yi Hong (14)	98
Helen Stewart (13)	99
Priya Floyd (14)	100
Anne Higgins (14)	101
Rachel Cooper (17)	102
Helen McEwan (14)	103
Danielle Grayston (12)	104
Darshikah Gnanakumar (12)	105
Jessica Sumping (12)	106
Catherine Branter (11)	107
Kathryn Griffiths (13)	108
Wajeeha Ahmed (12)	109
Hannah Tiernan (11)	110

The Poems

The Magic Box

(Based on 'Magic Box' by Kit Wright)

I will put in my box . . .
The soft gurgle of a beautiful newborn baby
The loud, terrifying bang of a firework
The glimmering spark of the hot sun

I will put in my box . . .
The ten last words of a dying young man
The first soft chew of a chewy pork chop
The first touch of boiling hot water on a freezing cold day

I will put in my box . . .
The first exciting word of a scary book
The wafting smell of crispy bacon cooked in the frying pan
The first warm sip of a nice cup of hot chocolate

I will put in my box . . .
A refreshing sip of freezing cold water on a boiling hot day
The ear-splitting roar of a brand new Ferrari
The first beautiful photo of a cheerful baby

I will put in my box . . .
The happy grin on a newborn baby's face
The sound of popcorn popping loudly
The cheer of somebody winning the lottery

I will put in my box . . .
An F1 driver in a boat and a sailor in an F1 car
The high jump of a turtle and the slow step of a kangaroo
The crunch of a drink and a sip of food

My box is made of fire, water and tin
With music on the lid and stories in the corners
Its hinges are made from the jaw bones of a fish

I will skydive into my box . . .
Spinning and somersaulting
Sailing through the sky
And land on a field of wonderful green grass
The colour of shiny emeralds.

Stefan Richards (10)

The Beach

The splashing waves rocking about like a battle commencing,
The shuffling sand swarming across the beach,
The cunning crabs relaxing in the rock pools,
The chattering fish meandering in the ocean.

As the moon disappears the sun arrives,
People start to fill the beach,
Children playing, adults relaxing and everyone having fun,
Eating, chatting, swimming and more all rolled into one.

The day is now ending and people start leaving,
The children are complaining because they don't want to go,
The fish go to sleep, the crabs have a snooze,
The sand stops shuffling and the waves calm down.

The magical sunset shows off his colours,
Red, yellow and orange,
Going down in a fantastic blaze,
Without a warning the sunset has gone and the night has come again.

Hollie Gilbody (11)
Coombe Girls' School

11 Days, 11 Ways

11 days, 11 ways,
11 chances, 11 says,
11 names but no 11 goodbyes,
11 memories with 11 sighs.

11 birds lost in thought,
11 mothers completely distraught,
11 my love it came too soon,
11 souls ordered to doom.

11 times lost with 11 songs,
11 people gone for which their heart longs,
11 days after the start,
11 worlds fell apart.

Phoebe Lindsley (11)
Coombe Girls' School

My Family

My grandad is a footballer,
Thinks he's Michael Owen,
My grandma is a pop star,
Instead of doing sewin'.

My auntie is a zookeeper,
Looks after all the monkeys,
My uncle is a factory worker,
Wraps up KitKat Chunkies.

My father is a teacher,
Teaches sums like 1+1,
My mother is a childminder,
Lets children have fun.

Who knows what the future will hold for me,
A scientist, a nurse, a football referee!

Emma Crutcher (11)
Coombe Girls' School

I'll Never Forget Your Face

You were once always beside me,
You were once always there,
You would follow me like a shadow,
You would always care.

Then one day you went away from me,
For what reason, I'm not sure why,
All I know is that day was sad for me
And made a tear fall from my eye.

But I still remember your loving heart,
No one can take your place,
You may be a distant memory,
But I'll never forget your face.

Michelle Ingham (11)
Coombe Girls' School

September The 11th

Panic-stricken cries of fear constantly reverberating,
The roaring of death's angel growing ever nearer,
Men and women leaping from the shaking building,
The face of the Earth growing clearer,
In those last terrible moments of their life let our hearts be with them.

The crashing as the planes hit,
Consumed in the billows of smoke,
Candles at the gates of Heaven are lit,
Gone are the last ashes of hope,
Darkness envelops them, may their souls find rest.

The flaring buildings explode with light,
People screaming and choking everywhere,
Rubble falling from a deadly height,
Whining sirens pierce the air,
Our anguish for the innocent runs deep in our hearts.

The black heart of terrorism, evil and cursed,
Tears beloved families apart,
The innocent victims confront the worst,
The doomed leave their farewells and then depart,
Why does such wickedness pollute the Earth? Let us stand united.

Let us support those who have lost their dear ones
And ensure nothing as catastrophic occurs again,
Now let us give thanks for every breath of life in our lungs,
And mourn the loss of those who were so cruelly slain,
May all of our hearts be with them
And that they at least have found peace.

Chlöe Fuller (11)
Coombe Girls' School

The Trees' Lament

I know a secret forest,
Full of trees and colourful birds
And the trees at the midnight hour
In the wind, whisper the words . . .

'They are coming,
They are near,'
And in the morning,
Came their fear.

Machines then entered the forest,
Crushing trees like a child with ants,
Like a herd of angry rhinos,
Came the pistons as the engine pants.

One by one fell the trees,
Destroying the homes of many
And then there is nothing for the creatures and birds,
Like a beggar who lived by a penny.

There was a secret forest,
Now there are only remains.

Harriet Hirschler (11)
Coombe Girls' School

A Girl's Dream

The glistening afternoon sun,
The sky like a watercolour,
The palest cold blue,
Velvet-green vines, a crystal clear shimmering lake,
The scent of a baby-pink rose
And a magical princess in her emerald castle.
The girl skips along the grey-stoned path
And enjoys a tea party with the fairies and magical princess,
What a wonderful garden, a beautiful place to be!

Lydia Ryan (11)
Coombe Girls' School

My Family

I know they're always there for me,
I know that they're around,
I can tell them all my secrets,
Because I know they'll keep them sound.
They know I'll always love them,
Till the day I die,
They know I'll always comfort them,
Every time they cry.

I know we sometimes argue,
Sometimes we disagree,
But in the end I always know,
That they're there for me,
In anything I do,
I know that they'll support me,
We're a very happy family,
It's obvious to see.

Kate Graves (11)
Coombe Girls' School

Life

Never is it appreciated,
Until it disappears,
It never stops bringing happiness,
But causes all tears.

The people that are afraid,
Love it too much,
They can be cursed by it,
With just one touch.

If you're not careful with it,
It will pierce through you like a knife,
The thing I am talking about,
Is, of course, life.

Charlotte Kelly (11)
Coombe Girls' School

Summer Holiday

Here comes summer,
I can't wait to go away,
The last day of school has come,
It's time for our holiday.

I helped Mum pack our suitcase
And drag it to the car,
'Are we nearly there yet?'
'No dear, we haven't gone far.'

We finally arrive,
I head straight for the pool,
With one big splash, I'm in there,
The water's really cool.

Dad takes us to the sandy beach,
I buy a bucket and spade,
We build a great big sandcastle,
The biggest we've ever made.

Fish 'n' chips and ice cream,
My favourite seaside meal,
Stripy rock and candyfloss,
'Mum, I do feel ill.'

Dad fell asleep on the deckchair,
With his hanky on his head,
Mum rubbed suncream on my back,
To stop me going red.

We went back to the caravan,
With sand between our toes,
Chocolate cake and tuna fish,
On holiday anything goes.

The seven days passed quickly
And now it's time to go,
Maybe we'll come back next year?
Oh, I do hope so!

Sarah Hilsum-White (11)
Coombe Girls' School

Inside

What's inside behind that door?
I want to go in to find out more,
But I can't, who knows what's in there,
A tiny mouse or a massive bear?

Here I am still right at the start,
Something's racing, it's my heart,
Going through the candlelit hall,
I can see shadows, small and tall.

I heard a crack and quickly whizzed round,
There in front of me, on the floor I found,
A small note, this is what it said,
'Go inside' scribbled in red.

My head is rushing with lots of thoughts,
Good ones, bad ones, some worse than warts.
What was I to do? I squeezed my book
And went inside to take a look!

Maryam Sadiq (11)
Coombe Girls' School

September Eleventh

September eleventh,
The day for disaster.
At nine o'clock;
It ended much faster.

All adult and child,
Harmed more than one way,
The catastrophe lives on,
Till this very day.

The Americans declared,
The culprits they'd pursue,
In agony in war;
From this world issue.

Victoria Nice (11)
Coombe Girls' School

Snowman

I saw him standing there this morning,
In the snow-carpeted garden,
I saw him standing there mourning,
I felt sorry for him standing there alone.

For inside that frozen snow,
I knew there was a frozen heart,
It was clear, obvious, I know,
Everyone felt sorry for him standing there alone.

Late morning the next day,
The sun shone through the clouds,
I knew it was going to play today,
I felt sorry for him melting there alone.

For inside that melting snow,
I knew there was a melting heart,
It was clear, obvious, I know,
Everyone felt sorry for him melting there alone.

Sophie Webb (12)
Coombe Girls' School

Ballerina

Soft tapping on the wooden floor,
A little pause and then some more,
The skin is baby-pink and fair,
The swish of an arm through the air,
Short gasps echo the small hall,
You can hear something inside silently fall.
A gust of wind flies through the window,
Pushing open the door,
Revealing what's inside;
A ballerina on the floor.

Katie Knichal (14)
Coombe Girls' School

My Pet

I asked Mum for a hamster
She said, 'Oh no, they stink'
I once bought home a goldfish
But she washed it down the sink

I asked Mum for a budgie
She said, 'Oh no, they talk'
I once bought home a spider
But it went out for a walk

I asked Mum for a pussycat
She said, 'Oh no, they scratch'
I once bought home a turtle's egg
But then it wouldn't hatch

Please Mum, can I have a pet?
I'll buy it with my money
I'll look after it and buy the food
If you let me have a bunny.

Bernadette Travers (11)
Coombe Girls' School

Autumn

The colours of a sunset fall from the trees, foggy grey mists
                                     lurking in the distance.
Waiting, waiting to swallow up a lost unsuspecting creature.
Hush, the darkness is arriving.
Watch God lay a black velvet coat over the evening sunset.
See the sparkling diamonds glisten above.
Hear the owl hooting, breaking the silence, shattering it like glass.
Awake! For I hear the lark call,
Dew glistens on the grass.
Frost lies upon the tops of cars, pointed and jagged.
Jack Frost has done his work.
Now all will be forgotten of that last autumn night.
It has been buried in snow, preserved for next year.
Though it is the winter now, it will soon be near.

Holly Aldous (11)
Coombe Girls' School

My Flute

Circular keys crown
Its long, delicate body
Shimmering silver

Air whispering through
Its slim cylindrical shape
Singing out its tune

Music rippling like
A gently flowing river
Fills the silent air

My fingers caress the keys
My mouth blows down the
Head joint's open hole

As I play my heart soars
My mind feels out of this world
This is my flute!

Rachel Mattick (11)
Coombe Girls' School

Optimism

Death scares but kills only few,
As angels are made by those like me and you,
If consumed by hate, guilt or betrayal,
You are likely to end happiness and continue to fail,
By not thinking of sadness or trying times,
Happiness will follow like the sun shines,
Your rain clouds will go and never return,
Inside yourself you'll continue to learn,
By getting the best out of you and your life,
Good times will follow avoiding any strife,
Be happy with yourself inside and out,
Realise what life is truly about,
If you continue to be happy and strong,
I can promise you this:
You will live long.

Sophie Ann Eastop (13)
Coombe Girls' School

The Dream Catcher

The dream catcher dangles above her bed
With colourful feathers and sparkling thread.
A circular frame and spiderweb design
Decorative little bows in a pretty line.

And there it sways to the air stream,
Simply waiting till she starts to dream
And when she does the dream catcher shines
And shimmers in the moonlight's dusty line.

It catches dreams of ocean rage,
Swirling whirlpools and tidal waves
Dark as the night the sinister sea
Catching the dreams of both you and me.

It catches the dreams of the countryside,
Large oak trees where rabbits hide,
Gliding birds up in the sky
Catching dreams from where we lie.

It catches dreams from out of space
Of different planets the comets grace.
The twinkling stars the rockets there
Catching the dreams of what we dare.

It catches dreams of mountains tall,
Of crumbling cliffs and waterfall
Of sleet and snow the wind that sweeps
Catching dreams from where we sleep.

It catches dreams of buried treasure
Searching in all types of weather
Of glistening jewels pirates that died
Catching the dreams of what's inside.

The dream catcher ceases when she stirs
And the sun sparkles through the glass windows
Then it goes back to its original form
And the dreams are let free into the dawn.

The dreams float away until night falls
Then enter children's hearts, minds and souls
More people dream the very same dream
And the dream catcher once more through the night gleams.

Rebecca Edwards (12)
Coombe Girls' School

Skiing

You're racing down the hill,
The wind upon your face,
Flying through the snow all around,
You're going way too fast,
You're about to hit a tree,
Closer, your heart begins to pound.

Bend your knees,
Open your eyes,
That was a close shave,
Here's the hill,
Looks too steep,
You have to be very brave.

You're nearly at the end,
Just past the final bend,
You can feel the snow drops and the breeze,
You're winning, you're winning,
Your head's spinning, it's spinning,
You can see the finish line, just beyond the trees.

Bethan Robinson (11)
Coombe Girls' School

The Moanings

The sun shines down
On a barren wasteland of nothing.
All the trees are being taken
Away on trucks and lorries.
The animals are left stranded
Watching the humans steal their home.

The rivers dry up to biscuit,
A drought has come on the land.
The trees are gone
And the animals too.
The rain will not come to wash
Away the sadness

The bulldozers come,
The bulldozers go.
The animals have left.
This is no longer their home.

Hannah Ilett (11)
Coombe Girls' School

Fog

Driving in the pouring rain on a gloomy December night
Wandering through the deserted street in mist as thick as snow
Dull trees stand as straight as boards and fog as white as cheeks
Cold air breathing on me

As I sleep, the mist and fog grows, crawling on my face
Spreading over my hair and my eyes thick with sleep
I can only see the ghostly mist as it fills my room like water
Making my bedclothes fly off

It's morning now, the fog has gone only accidents show he was there
Piled up cars, battered and worn, the air now soft and warm
Not frozen cool and shrill, now it's warm and soft
It has gone!

Rachel Luck (12)
Coombe Girls' School

Winter Snow

Winter snow is a magical gift,
Past the window we watch it drift.

Winter snow is really cold,
But it's something children love to hold.

Winter snow falls lightly from the sky,
Like sugar dusting on a warm apple pie.

Winter snow lets children sledge and ski
And fills the atmosphere with happiness and glee.

Winter snow is so much fun,
Akin to the joy of the hot summer sun.

Winter snow shines so soft and white,
It looks outside like a midsummer's night.

Winter snow settles across the lands,
Sugary sprinkles in children's hands.

Winter snow covers the frozen lake,
Like perfect icing on a perfect cake.

Sophie Wheeler (11)
Coombe Girls' School

The Poor Old Man!

One summer's day in the middle of winter,
The moon shone bright in the day.
The dog went miaow and the cat went woof,
But the old man had nothing to say!

The stars were out and the sun was too,
The dog climbed up the tree.
The cat flew high and the bird swam low
And a chicken galloped home for its tea!

The old man stopped, a little bemused
And looked up to the sky,
He sighed very slowly and felt very lonely,
When a fish poked him in the eye!

Emily Wheeler (12)
Coombe Girls' School

Anger Is . . .

Anger is hatred bottled up inside
Anger is when you can't swallow your pride
Anger is screaming without any sound
Anger is when you're plummeting down
Anger is a flood of suppressed pain
Anger is annoyance throbbing through your veins
Anger is cutting someone with a sharp tongue
Anger is shooting with your eyes as a gun
Anger is burning with words of hate
Anger is feeling trapped and irate
Anger is vowing to get revenge
Anger is feeling a burning twinge
Anger is hearing a roaring in your ears
Anger is being blind to your fear
Anger is tasting bitterness in your mouth
Anger is making helplessness and strife
Anger is learning to swim through despair
And anger is learning to rise like air . . .

Sinéad Morrison (13)
Coombe Girls' School

Winter

I creep in like a mischievous robber,
Nicking the leaves from the terrified trees,
I bare an icy white cloak, sweeping it over everything,
As I leap over a carpet of snow, I scare away the southbound birds,
Welcoming the robins into my care.
I prepare groovy discos for flames in fireplaces
And as they dance they flicker and twist,
My fun is almost over; I get angry and conjure up a blizzard,
Each delicate flake being whisked away by the deafening wind.
But now I must go, for as my time ends, the spring's time begins,
I flee, scared for my life of fog and mist,
As I leave I see the first fragile flower grow,
The first blue tit sing and prepare for my adventure once again!

Emily Adams (11)
Coombe Girls' School

My English Homework

I've been told to write a poem
About what I don't quite know,
I'm sure my teacher would like to see
All that I can show.

Have you any ideas
Of what I should pen down,
To make my teacher smile
And fade away her frown?

Various subjects come to mind
Of dogs, cats or bees,
What would you say was your vote
On any one of these?

Perhaps you would like nice fragrant flowers
Or maybe a witch with evil, magical powers?

Time is ticking on; I don't know what to do,
It's really quite frustrating and I'm taking it out on you!
Sorry for the anger,
But to my teacher's whims I must pander.

There is no point in sitting here,
For all this time has gone
And still there is no subject
For me to get cracking on.

You're absolutely useless, you're no help at all
And now I have no one else left to call.

Now it's getting late and I'm in big trouble
And my poem looks more like a pile of rubble.

I've spent all day and I bet I won't get an A,
Because I'm still tyring to find a subject on something I cay say!

Marium Sallah (11)
Coombe Girls' School

Weather Haikus

Snow is soft and white,
The crunch brings joy to my heart,
But snow is so rare.

Rain is quite like snow,
Except rain is not so cold,
But I hate it loads.

Sun is very fun,
The sun brings much joy to me,
For I can go out.

When wind blows its top,
The air turns so very cold,
Yet sometimes it's warm.

When fog screens my eyes
And the world is lost in white,
The mist floods my mind.

Humid is awful,
It completely blocks my mind
And makes me sweaty.

When hail rains down hard
And it is scary outside,
I love my warm house.

Red, yellow, orange,
The rainbow enters the sky,
But soon it says bye.

A strong gust of wind,
The tornado strikes the land
And destroys the homes.

Splish, splash, crash and scream,
The tidal wave rises up,
Splosh goes this poem.

Heather Rolfe (11)
Coombe Girls' School

Revelation

The sun was a burning moon on scarlet waves
To signal the end of this world of knaves.
The wind was harsh as if full of nails.
The heavens and hells were bound only by phantom veils.

In the skies, clear as blades, were four riders on beasts of flame.
I stood paralytic, too fearful to flee, and could only watch
                                        as they came.
They dragged behind them a darkness that divided as a swarm.
This grew as the seconds passed and the adversary took his form.

Even mortals could sense the thoughts of this shadow
                                        of malevolence.
Then a light pierced through this cloud, our almighty benevolence.
'Take this warning,' declared Metatron, 'for Lucifer, you shalt not win.
You of all the fallen should know that God will always conquer sin.'

Satan, once an angel, laughed, a sound that melodied terrible things.
'Beelzebub, Azrael, come to me,' the Devil called, unfolding his wings.
He glowed with heathen fire, with a beauty that only evil can possess.
He wanted to claim, wanted control, and he would settle
                                        for nothing less.

Lightning illuminated all; the ground beneath me tore.
Hordes and hordes of demons scrabbled through the earthen floor.
Teeth of swords, eyes of pits, these were the unholy damned.
They rose from the confinements in which they had been
                                        trapped and crammed.

Angels stood in righteous ranks, always resonating calm and grace.
Yet, none of them assembled there showed mercy in their face.
The lowly people on Earth panicked, like chickens in their coops.
But I knew that there was nowhere that one could hide
                                        from these troops.

The flaw with the 'divine' plan is that it aims to prove our worth.
However, it was not designed for the cares of man, and will lay
                                        waste the Earth.

Louise Champion (15)
Coombe Girls' School

The Amateur Poet

She sits with drawn and melancholy face
Juggling potential lines with grim despair
Bleak, searching eyes stare glassily to space
And brokenly she moans, 'This isn't fair!'
With falt'ring haste she attempts to compose
A sonnet that will set the world at peace
As time slips by her sense of panic grows
She tries her mute ideas to release
Then suddenly she laughs, in triumph grins
At what appears to be divine insight
With placid satisfaction she begins
The tale of a wild and gruesome fight
Briefly she revels in the death and pain
Then snorts, crosses it out and starts again

She struggles to express the latest thought
That must be snared within a wordy cage
The image sparkles up, but when it's caught
It gradually withers on the page
At length, with many a deep grimace and frown
In time, with many a concentrating grunt
She, on her laptop, tries to write it down
Which proves to be a Herculean stunt
This line won't scan, this word she cannot spell
And even when she finally completes it
She's plunged into still further depths of Hell
When, through some fatal mishap, she deletes it!
With one last, painful choke her muse expires
And, cursing her computer, she retires.

Katherine Miller (14)
Coombe Girls' School

I Wish I Could Fly

'A caterpillar am I,
But oh, how I wish I could fly,'
Little Wriggle said to the bee.
'I wish I had wings like you,
I wish I could fly like you do,
This is my dream you see.'
Said the bee to Little Wriggle,
(With a bit of a giggle!)
'You'll be flying very soon,
You'll make you a home,
Where you'll live all alone
And this will be called your cocoon,
When you're ready
And when you're steady,
Out you'll come,
You'll have wings of blue
Or yellow or maroon,
Ready to flap and have fun!'
'So *I* will be a butterfly
And I could fly way up high?
I could be a papillon flying around in France,
On the French, fluffy clouds, I will dance
Or I could be a kelebek,
Flying over the Turkish sea.
What a beautiful sight it would be.
We could fly there, you and me!'
Little Wriggle smiled,
'You have made my wish come true!
My best friend ever is you.
Thank you!'

Sophie Beadle (13)
Coombe Girls' School

The Four Seasons Haikus

Spring is the season
When the flowers open up,
In the warm sunshine.

Lambs are frolicking,
All of the birds are cheeping
And that is springtime.

Summer's the season
When we all go far away,
To the sunny beach.

Fun and games all day,
Who has time to work, just play,
Jumping all around.

The autumn is here,
Scrunching around in the leaves,
Time for harvesting.

Nights are long and cold,
Hallowe'en is drawing near,
Witches, ghosts and ghouls.

Winter is the time
When the snow is falling down
And laughter is here.

Christmas is now near,
Lots of presents, lots of food,
The winter has gone.

A year has now passed,
Spring, summer, autumn, winter,
Time for the next spring.

Emily Bowers-Clark (11)
Coombe Girls' School

Tomorrow Never Comes

Tomorrow never comes
No matter what you say
You could struggle to reach it
You could wait all day

Tomorrow is a place
That you can't really touch
It's always one step further
It's always from your clutch

It's a place of mysteries
Waiting to be found
It's a hole of surprises
Deep down in the ground

It's the place of all places
It's the king of all kings
It's the start of new life
It's full of magical things

But as hard as you try
No matter what you say
Tomorrow never comes
It's always another today.

Rebekah Jones (11)
Coombe Girls' School

The Creature In The Bath

It creeps and crawls
Then slips and falls
And moves with its eight long legs

It scuttles and trails
Then slips and fails
The creature in the bath!

It moves up and down
Then falls to the ground
Its journey never ceases

It moves more and more
Then falls to the floor
The creature in the bath!

The plughole's in sight
The creature takes flight
And down the drain it goes

Falling down and down
And out - homebound
No creature in the bath!

Katharine Bracey (11)
Coombe Girls' School

Crocodile

Deep in a swamp lives an animal,
With teeth as sharp as blades.
Waiting . . . waiting for its prey,
Hungry, hungry,
Wait! . . . It sees something above,
Sneaking . . . sneaking until the time is right and . . .
Snap!

Victoria Coppen (12)
Dunottar School

The Bear

In the stream are silver fish
And how I always wish,
That hunters would understand
That this is the bear's land.

He roams the forest free,
As strong as he can be,
As black as the darkest night,
He is an awesome sight.

He can be very dangerous,
For I know he is courageous,
He takes only what he needs,
For he has no greed.

In the stream are silver fish
And how I always wish,
That hunters would understand,
That this is the bear's land.

Kathryn Miles (13)
Dunottar School

The Tigers

T he tigers creep along the shadowed path
H eaving through the damp, damp grass
E ating and sleeping in the migrating heat

T he jungle is sticky while they're on their feet
I t is very hard for where they are
G nawing bones was a lovely meal
E xercise is very easy for them to do
R apidly running, now that's the thing to do
S lowly tiring, time to go to bed.

Rezwana Hussain (11)
Dunottar School

In The Jungle

I went one day to see the animals
    I couldn't believe my eyes,
I walked along a very big field,
    For what seemed like miles.

I moved very close to a cluster of trees,
    Into an enormous ditch
And look over there, there's a panther,
    Catching a poor little bird.

I was just about to run over there,
    When I saw a hoof,
These animals were going to jump on me,
    If I had not moved.

I walked a few yards
    To see a huge tiger,
A snake and a parrot
    My friends wouldn't want to see either.

Danniella Schindler (11)
Dunottar School

The Painted Lady!

She gracefully flutters through the trees,
Her magnificent colours of autumn leaves;
So elegant and fine,
The colours of her wings, divine;
She wanders through forests, she only knows,
Flying by the waterfall where the river flows;
Dancing in the fading light,
Swifting like a children's kite;
Before merging into her blossom tree
And so to sleep, so tranquilly,
She settles softly.

Larissa Brett (11)
Dunottar School

Wishing For A Cat

Long-haired, short-haired,
Ginger or tabby,
Tomcat or female,
What would I choose?

Perhaps a white Persian,
All fluffy and soft
Or a little black kitten,
To bring me good luck.

I would so love a cat,
But my dad isn't keen,
He says, 'Think of the fur balls,
Vet bills and fleas.'

'Just keep on asking,'
Is my mum's advice,
'Perhaps try telling him
We would never have mice.'

They're really no bother,
They sleep all the day
And Grandma would feed it,
When we are away.

I'll try a bit longer
And if I can't turn his head,
Perhaps I'll ask for a pony instead.

Lucy Houlding (11)
Dunottar School

Seasons

Leaves are turning crisp and gold,
Trees are bare, leafless and cold.
As I go along the main road,
I hear the crunchy leafy load.

It changes to winter as trees turn white,
After five, it's no longer light.
Snowballs are flying in the air,
Snowmen look like Tony Blair.

Here comes spring as birds come along,
The town is filled with their merry song.
The flowers are blossoming with their pretty petals,
Out of the ground sprout naughty nettles.

At last it's summer which brings joyful shouts,
The street is filled with careless louts.
The children are no longer in school,
They have their break in a calming cold pool.
Some go on vacation, some fly away,
But I, the author, am lying at the bay!

Aileen Doyle (11)
Dunottar School

My First Day

The day is here, all bright and sunny,
So why does my tummy feel so funny?
I'm all dressed and ready and it's time to go,
I'm in the car, 'Oh Mum, please go slow.'

I arrive at the door and open it slowly,
There are so many girls, I feel quite lonely.
I know I have a buddy, where can she be?
'Hello,' says a girl, 'are you new? Follow me.

'I'm your buddy, my name is Lucy Day,
Your classroom's through here, you'll soon know the way.
Don't look so worried,' she says with a smile.
'You'll make friends really fast, it will only take a short while.'

She was right you know,
I've settled in well,
The work is sometimes tricky,
But my new school and new friends are brill!

Rosie Case-Green (11)
Dunottar School

The Panda

A panda collapsed among a bed of bamboo
And started munching his crunchy lunch,
The bamboo grew tall, slim and straight,
As if pencils surrounded the big black and white giant.
Off he moved to the water so clear
And slurped as he peers into the water so deep,
Along the broken stalk road he went,
As if a man was plodding through the puddles,
One rainy day.
The panda carried on through the monkey's lair
And then arrived at his cave,
Then collapsed among a bed of bamboo.

Camilla Lambert (11)
Dunottar School

Silver Sprint

Sometimes
If you look closely
You can almost see
Silver shapes
Sprinting through long
Peppermint-green grass
Hooves tiptoeing

They can see you but
You can't really see them
Think, where would they hide?
Almond-shaped eyes
Empty and hollow.

Dark shadows looming
Human breath
A crunch of a leaf . . .
Argh
I've been given away
Shall I show myself?

Trotting under the midnight sky
Stars twinkling so high
A silver shape

What am I?

Ellie Preston (11)
Dunottar School

The Red Admiral

T here once was a red admiral
H er wings were as red as flames
E merging from her chrysalis to arise with the new day

R ed admiral's beauty was like no other
E very butterfly adored her
D ainty wings and gracious movements as she silently
                                        crossed the sky

A queen among her kind
D etermined to stay up high
M ajestically ruling the meadows
 I n the hazy sunshine
R ain makes her shelter beneath a leaf
A utumn comes too quickly
L eaves cover her body as she takes her final breath.

Everlyn Perry-Mason (11)
Dunottar School

What Is The Meaning Of Life?

What is the meaning of life?
Is it to get a good job
Or a husband or a wife?
I wonder what is the meaning of life?
Is it to stand up for your rights
And have a choice?
The meaning of life is your choice!

Luke Emilianou (13)
Glenthorne High School

Why Me?

While I live on these cold streets
All I hear are people's feet
Rushing by to work and home
I wonder why I'm so alone
Some people seem to stop and stare
Which makes me wonder, do they care?
As I lay inside my box
For food I rummage like a fox
To live like them I need a chance
Will someone give me a second glance
Some people think that we are trash
Because we pray and beg for cash
I should not have to live this way
I hope this is my lucky day.

Daniel Illman (12)
Glenthorne High School

My Little Doom

Oh no, can't you see?
Loneliness is getting to me
Sitting here freezing cold
Feeling like I will collapse and fold

The atmosphere is creepy and bitter
I am surrounded by litter
It's not grand, it's not sweet
It definitely smells of feet
Yes, that's right, it's my own little doom
My room!

Carmella Carmichael (12)
Glenthorne High School

Man On The Moon

I always lay awake at night
the moon just seems so far and bright

Sometimes I begin to dream and wonder
which always makes me even fonder

I wish it's somewhere beyond the stars
somewhere, somehow it's very far

I look out of my window and begin to stare
but on the sun he's not there

I look on Mars, it's still burning
I can't see well because Earth is turning

I look at Pluto, it looks very cold
or that's just what I've been told

Venus looks like the planet of love
from where I am sitting, I see one white dove

On Neptune I see it's brewing a storm
with rain and lightning, not very warm

I'm so bored, I begin to sigh
but then I look one more time

I look closer with my eye
what is this? To my surprise

I've finally seen the
man on the moon.

Sophia Jeddaoui (12)
Glenthorne High School

Decisions

What do you do in the evenings
now that winter has begun?
We could watch television,
but playing games is fun.

But what games do we play?
That is the question,
It's a really hard choice,
has anyone got a suggestion?

Uno, darts and Battleships,
Checkers, Scrabble or Cluedo,
Bingo, mah-jong or conkers,
tiddlywinks, Draughts or Ludo.

Masterpiece, Chess or Monopoly,
Dominoes, colditz or cards,
The Game of Life or rummikub,
skittles, dice or charades.

By the time someone has chosen
it will be time for bed,
if nobody can make their mind up
we'll all watch telly instead.

Michael Lewis (13)
Glenthorne High School

A Fright In The Night

While you are tucked up fast asleep,
Skeletons walk and make you creep.

But don't take fright,
When it's scary at night.

Ghosts walk down your halls
And creep through the walls,
Don't worry yourselves,
When heads sit on your shelves.

But don't take a fright,
When it's scary a night.

When the mice come out,
The witches scream and shout,
They use small white feathers,
To tickle your nose,
Whilst frogs sit on the end of your nose.

But don't take a fright,
When it's scary at night.

Katie Wakefield
Glenthorne High School

Football

F ootball, football, it's the best
O n cup final day I'll beat the rest
O pen goal, will I score?
T aken down, I'm on the floor
' B ut that was a foul ref,' I say
A nd then I moan in dismay
L ots of people gather round, I'm in real pain
L ooking at me as if I'm insane!

Josh Perry (13)
Glenthorne High School

The Storm

The storm is roaring,
The trees are shaking,
The stallion stands still,
As it tries to find shelter,
Through the pouring rain,
It believes in just *hope*,
For hope is all it has.

Hours pass,
The storm doesn't,
The white horse becomes startled,
By the rumble of the thunder
And the flashes of the lightning,
It can no longer stand its ground,
The forest becomes flooded.

Water arises,
In the hope to find Heaven,
Only it's not the stream that will find it,
The stallion is drowning,
It struggles to reach higher grounds,
But it's not too late,
The stallion gives all its strength
And has one last go on life.

The storm stops,
The horse is now safe,
He made it,
It slowly breathes in deep breaths
And at last gallops home,
Where it is warm, safe and storm-free!

Lauren Brown (12)
Glenthorne High School

My Little Star

You were my little star,
But you were too far.
You shone so clear and bright,
In the so little light.

Tonight I think,
I saw you wink,
As if to say 'Goodnight'.

If I see you,
Can you see me,
With your twinkling eye?

You were my little star,
But you were too far.
You shine so clear and bright,
In the so little light.

I love my little star,
But he has grown,
So he's not my little star,
He is my big star!

Emily Blight (11)
Glenthorne High School

Love

I leave you now
Longing to have you in my arms again
Not knowing when I'll see you next
I might go insane

Unknowingly you're causing me this uncomfortable pain
For you I lose my sight
I have no shame
I hear a song and think of your name

But to get you, I'm not enough
You want fame, the way things go it's so unfair
You called my name and I was there
I needed you and you weren't anywhere

Now I'm thinking, *do you even care?*
Was it all just a prank? A dare?

You're playing with my heart
Seeming so unaware
Your feelings hidden always
Mine I'll always share
So now I look in your eyes
With a longing stare.

Francine Taylor (13)
Glenthorne High School

My Dreams

When I fall into a deep sleep,
I always have weird dreams,
My eyes never open, not even a peep,
Everything looks so real, but nothing is what it seems.

As my dream becomes my fantasy,
My eyes begin to overflow,
My mum is telling me to wake up,
But I don't want to, I say, 'No.'

My fantasy is drifting away,
I guess I might as well get up,
Gotta go to school,
I must hurry so I gulp my cup.

I'm at school and what a joy it is,
I'm already late for sleeping in too long,
I look such a state and my hair is just a pile of frizz.

School is over and I come back to my bed,
Every part of my body hurts especially my heavy head,
Again I fall into a deep sleep,
But in this dream there are angels with me,
They take me to Heaven and tell me to always look on
The bright side of life,
Night-night, sleep tight.

Abbie Reuben (12)
Glenthorne High School

My Poem

I hate poetry,
It's just so boring.

I did this homework,
When day was dawning.

I wrote four lines
And started snoring.

I find it hard,
To stop myself yawning.

They gave this homework,
Without any warning.

That's why I got up and
Did it this morning.

Leigh Henthorn (12)
Glenthorne High School

The Girlie Group

I have a girlie group,
We are all best mates,
We fill each other in about
Make-up, fashions and dates.

We meet up at playtime,
To have a girlie goss,
There's Stacie, Cassie, Natasha, me
And Lauren, she's the boss.

We make up and break up all the time,
It really is quite mad,
We giggle in assembly and classes,
Which really is quite bad!

It's fun to have best friends,
On who we can rely,
We'll be friends forever,
We'll never say goodbye.

Zennia Camille Coombs (13)
Norbury Manor High School for Girls

War And Peace

We don't need war,
We need the peace.
We need to be nicer,
To the people that we meet.

We don't need war,
We need the peace.
We don't want homeless people,
Living on the streets.

We don't need war,
We need the peace,
We need a good shelter,
For the homeless people to sleep.

We don't need war,
We need the peace,
People are dying,
Even in Greece.

We don't need war,
We need the peace,
We need to stop the war,
For there to be peace.

Bindiya Dhanak (13)
Norbury Manor High School for Girls

Something You Should Know

Feel sluggish and slow,
    Feel like there's something you should know.

These genetic heroin addicts
    Won't leave me alone.
        I guess that's because I jumped the red light

. . . And now I'm driving

       . . . Driving away.

               Won't look back.

Turn on the TV and there's a judge,
He's telling me how much I suck

And I can feel him with his veinless arms,
Yeah, I think he knows
Where I live,   (I think he knows where I live.)

Turn on the kettle and all I smell is radium.
Got to clean the limescale

Staring like an OCD with a prime number in my head
Yeah I think

I'll go to bed with that man

The one I killed.
(The one I think I killed.)

These genetic heroin addicts
    Won't leave me alone.
        I guess then, that there's something you should know
               He wasn't my father or brother
               But I know him
               He sleeps next to me all night
               Smelling of the streets.

               And he drinks my milk with coco pops
               And he pays half of the bill.

               They don't know where he went that night

I still think back sometimes
        Wonder if they saw me skid away
                A black Mercedes   through an illegal red light
                                On a tarmac street

I thought I'd go back to redeem myself.

        Thought I'd go back to redeem myself.

                Thought I'd go back to redeem myself.

But I can't get rid of his hair.
        Every time I try the damn stuff
                Comes back   (it reappears)

They don't know who I am
Who he was or where he is
So there's something you should know,
        (There's something you should know.)

Jeneece Bernard (15)
Norbury Manor High School for Girls

Peace And War

It's pretty hard to live the life
When we hear the souls that died
God, please hear our cry
Tell them stop killing our lives
Life is too short for killing
Life is all about living
But how can we live the life
When there are terrorists
That are still alive?
Child, please don't cry
Your father is still alive
Think positive not negative
Because of this war
Our world is now
Ending!

Sheliza Ann Williams (13)
Norbury Manor High School for Girls

I Don't Know Where I'm Going But I Know How To Get There

I don't know where I'm going,
But I know how to get there.

I'm here lying in the rain,
I can afford a tent, I can't pay the rent.
I'm here slowly slipping away.
I live on my own breaths, with no regrets.
That's how I want it to stay.
I'm here breaking this silence.
The enigma's past. My future's cast.
I'm here minding my own problems.
I fall in that ditch, to scratch that itch.
I never liked that simple answer.

I can't see my stepping-stones,
But I know the river is around the corner.
I don't know where I'm going,
But I know how to get there.
I don't know where I'm going,
But I know how to get there.

I'm here looking out the window,
The sunlight blinds me. The rain never lets me free.
I'm here just longing to grow.
I live on my own seeds, to try and win the good deeds.
I have now got to go.
I'm here busting my homework.
I haven't got a clue. Does one and one equal two?
I'm here drowning in this dirt.
I've gone through so much pain, just to make me sane.
I can't afford this hurt.

I can't follow the yellow brick road,
Yet Oz is one train ride away.
I don't know where I'm going,
But I know how to get there.
I don't know where I'm going,
But I know how to get there.
I don't know where I'm going,
But I know how to get there.
I don't know where I'm going,
But I know how to get there.

Joe Lawrence (16)
Reigate College

Seeing Through The Mask

My lips are brutal when I speak the truth
I can be an angel . . . I can be a devil . . .
But when you think you've marked me
It's funny to learn that I was onto you all along . . .
You liked to see me crawl . . . but in the end it was you on the floor
I saw through you . . . I didn't understand but I saw it . . .
The true you . . . the demon within.

Samantha Tyrrell (17)
Reigate College

Dad

My eyes are heavy,
My head is torn,
My thoughts emerge
And then get lost.

Uncontrollable pictures,
Images which torment my mind,
The fan in the corner,
To keep his temperature kind.

His skin was so pure,
So clean and so soft,
His eyes so peaceful
And his breathing so dim.

The mask on his mouth,
The bed where he lay,
The needle that stabbed,
His pure soft skin.

That chair where I sat
And told him I loved him,
Where I rocked back and forth,
With nothing to say.

The tears on her face
And his and them,
Their tears on mine,
All showed our love.

Jennifer Pickett (17)
Reigate College

Sister

You sing in a funny little way, feeble and small
Usually a melancholy tune that touches us.
You tell me not to listen, it's for you,
I'm invading your retreat;

The invading clump eats into your body,
Corrodes into your faith in fairness,
You weep silently, I'm all the worse for it.
We cry, you reveal nothing,
Not despair or distaste for the blossoming flower
That burrows and furrows with its roots.
They plunge deep into your flesh
Your beautiful English rose skin
So pale now, frail now, a vulnerable sight you seem.
But you are strong, so much stronger than I,
Tolerantly you wait in fright,
Like the patient, patient you must be.

A reaction; I found you
Pounding at your chest last night,
Why has it settled itself here?
You're angry and exhausted.
Fragments of shattered hope
Are thrust into your eyes,
Bringing forward the salted beads of sadness
But the broken days keep passing.
The deep angry nothing has left you,
Despair flushes the anger in.
My voice seems in a vacuum,
You cannot hear, your courage is silenced,
Now you weep.

When you're singing that melancholy tune,
In your lonely bed we just sit here,
Hold you by the hand and stoke your soft face.
We let the thriving lump feed off your strength.

Anna Manvell (17)
Reigate College

Animals

Gerbils, horses, spiders, cats,
Camels, monkeys, donkeys, rats.
Dolphins, pandas, lions, whales,
Panthers, cheetahs, zebras, snails.
Fishes, robins, blackbirds, snakes,
Ravens, cockerels, chickens, apes.
Leeches, coral, rabbits, seals,
Tigers, ibex, lizards, eels.
Reindeer, starfish, turtles, cows,
Hedgehogs, starlings, blue tits, sows.
Otters, pheasants, adders, frogs,
Reptiles, beetles, beavers, dogs.
Mammals, oysters, scallops, crabs,
Muscles, foxes, dormice, dabs.
Haddock, salmon, lampreys, hares,
Rag worms, weasels, crickets, bears.

Kathryn Pendrous (11)
St Bede's School, Redhill

The Sea

Seaweed, mussel, limpet, cave,
Sea horse, jellyfish, dolphin, wave.

Sharks, crabs, coral, whale,
Cliff top, octopus, saltwater snail.

Squid, whelk, swimmer, gull,
Eel, angler, ship's hull.

Pollution, sand, angelfish, rocks,
Stingray, triggerfish, remains of old docks.

Manta ray, stonefish, barnacle, shell,
Lobster, bladder wrack, an ugly oil well.

William Payne (11)
St Bede's School, Redhill

The Recipe For A Human

An ounce of integrity,
A shortage of envy,
A dollop of humour,
A gram of friendship,
A tablespoon of charm,
A teaspoon of ambition,
A handful of calmness,
A pinch of competition,
A sprinkle of jealousy,
A vine of intelligence,
A gram of kindness,
A drizzle of radiance,
A grain of hate,
A scoop of generosity,
An ounce of faith,
A pinch of curiosity,
A tonne of gratitude,
A litre of personality,
A clump of warmth,
A cup of punctuality,
A really nice human
This will make,
That's if you don't do
A single mistake.

Sarah Isherwood (13)
St Bede's School, Redhill

You're As Useless . . .

You're as useless as a blank TV,
as a dry, waterless sea.
You're as useless as a mute radio,
as a mower that does not mow.

You're as useless as a hot igloo,
as a cow that does not moo.
You're as useless as a leaking house,
as a rich, lonely spouse.

You're as useless as a one-handed clock,
as a door that does not lock.
You're as useless as a black light bulb,
as a freezer that's not cold.

You're as useless as can be,
if only you were just like me!

Hayley Miles (14)
St Bede's School, Redhill

Mummy's Dressing Table

A mirror far bigger than me,
More drawers than fish in the sea,
Perfume bottles excite you,
Lipsticks stand tall above you,
The loose powder is consuming,
Mascara wands are enchanting,
Nail varnish colours lined up like soldiers,
Blusher brushes - peacocks' tails in showers,
Lipglosses scattered in piles,
Eyeshadows spreading for miles,
Brushes and combs, curlers and pins,
Small cotton wool balls thrown in the bin.

And a little stool just in front of where I watch Mummy,

Every morning.

Laura Shaw (13)
St Bede's School, Redhill

Shopaholic

Eggs, bacon
sausage rolls
sugar, flour
Barbie dolls

Chocolate sweets
herbal teas
pizzas, apples
frozen peas

Cherries, lettuce
shredded wheat
tomatoes, spinach
lump of meat

Butter, cabbage
strawberry swirls
gold, silver
shining pearls

Chinese 5 spice
mixed herbs
basil, thyme
books with blurbs

Rose, daisies
entangled vines
gin, brandy
white wines

Polos, Twix
candy bars
oil, shampoo
sparkling cars.

Patrick McKenna (11)
St Bede's School, Redhill

My Favourite Things

Chocolate, raisins,
tap and Guides,
music, fashion,
shops and rides.

Gerbils, dolphins,
lions and rats,
fishes, penguins,
puppies, cats.

Heather, tulips,
oak trees, roses,
daffodils, ivy,
buttercups, posies.

Baked beans, raisins,
chocolates, cakes,
yoghurts, apples,
pizza, steaks.

Seashells, rock pools,
crabs, sea mouse,
sea water, oysters,
caves, fish louse.

D-Side, Britney,
Ash, Liberty X,
Triple 8, Westlife,
N*Sync, Steps.

Chocolate, raisins,
tap and Guides,
music, fashion,
shops and rides.

Roisin Skinner (11)
St Bede's School, Redhill

Girly Stuff!

Girls love . . .

Curlers, roses
princess, castles

Varnish, Justin
birthday parcels

Lippy, flowers
purple, Maltesers

Leo, David
files and tweezers

Hairspray, brushes
shopping, daisies

Earrings, salons
Top Shop, babies

Gossip, music
money, Kickers

Scissors, crimpers
nails and knickers

Straighteners, facials
Pantene, scrunchies

Singing, Robbie
strawberries, bunchies

Rollers, Corrie
blusher, kittens

Bracelets, Duncan
Etam, mittens.

Melanie Failes (14)
St Bede's School, Redhill

You're As Useless As . . .

You're as useless as . . .
A window with no glass,
An orchestra with no brass.
A car with no wheels,
A chemist with no pills.
A class without a teacher,
A sermon without a preacher.
A house without a floor,
A wall without a door.
A wig with no hair,
A shop which is bare.
A mine without coal,
Shoes without a sole.
A garden without a shed,
A hotel without a bed.
A downfall with no rain,
A railway with no train.
A book with no pages,
A job with no wages.
A tongue with no words,
An aviary with no birds.
A restaurant with no meals,
Stilettos with no heels.
A road with no car,
A hole without a par.
A TV with no screen,
A yell without a scream.
A ding without a dong,
A ping without a pong.
Cotton with no threads,
Pencils with no leads.
You're as useless as . . .
You!

Richard Miles (14)
St Bede's School, Redhill

Cats!

Mouse killers
Bird eaters
Garden wreckers
Ankle nippers

Fish lovers
Cheese feasters
Fussy feeders
Loud speakers

Strong fighters
Little soldiers
Deadly hunters
Silent stalkers

Sly walkers
Crafty thinkers
Super washers
Mega groomers

Super jumpers
Speedy sprinters
Attention seekers
Wool tanglers
Happy sleepers!

Gareth Pettit (12)
St Bede's School, Redhill

Worthless

You're as worthless as a ten rupee voucher
as an empty bank account
as a pound stuck to the floor
as a toothless vampire count

You're as worthless as a pencil with no lead
as a football with no air
as a table with no legs
as a hitman that can care

You're as worthless as a shirt with no buttons
as a racehorse that is lame
as a phone with no numbers
as a candle with no flame

You're as worthless as a clock without the hands
as a fish without the sea
as a painter with no paint

You're worthless just like me!

I'm as worthless as a TV with no screen
as a dump without the mess
as a genie with no wish

It seems we're both worthless!

Danny St John-Hall (13)
St Bede's School, Redhill

You're As Useless As . . .

You're as useless as . . .
A circuit without a wire,
As a flame without a fire.
A book without a rack,
As a snake without a back.
A spaceman without a rocket,
As a coat without a pocket.
Elastic string without a ping,
As a dong without a ding.
A hand without its fingers,
As a choir without its singers.
A flower without a petal,
As a car without any metal.
A comb without its teeth,
As a sword without a sheath.
A pencil without its lead,
As a mattress without a bed.
A table without any pine,
As a mirror without any shine.
A crayon without any colour,
As some bread without any butter.

Jonathan Murphy (13)
St Bede's School, Redhill

Choices

Olives, caviar
Palma ham
Snails, roast beef
Gingers, jam

Pizza, French fries
Chocolate cake

Curry, burgers
Ice cream, flake

Champagne, Pimms
Sparkling wine

Beer, lager
Vodka and lime

Cola, Sprite
Lilt and Tango

Fanta, Powerade
Grape and mango.

Claudia Baxter (14)
St Bede's School, Redhill

Girls!

Secret diaries
Chocolate éclairs
Gossip, shopping
Giggling on chairs
Justin, pop
R'n'B
Romantic comedies
We like to see
Lipstick, powder
Blusher, gel
Fake tan, earrings
Clothes as well
Crimpers, highlights
Dyes and hair
Curlers, straighteners
Handle with care

Girls' dream night in
Guys' nightmare.

Abbie Parsons (11)
St Bede's School, Redhill

When I Grow Up, I Want To Be . . .

When I grow up, I want to be
A master of philosophy
A builder or a fairy queen
The captain of a submarine

I want to be a dentist too
Or else a monkey at the zoo
A banker, dancer or optician
Aladdin's genie, a musician

Maybe I'll be a fine princess
A swordsman, postman or actress
An author or IT technician
Manager or a wise magician

I want to be a fire-eater
Farmer, fireman, carpet beater
I don't know what I want to be
I suppose I'd better just be me.

Natalie Gill   (13)
St Bede's School, Redhill

You Are . . .

You're as useless	as a mountain with no top,
	as a start without a stop,
	as a rhyme without a reason,
	as a year without a season.

You're as boring as an actor with no talent,
as a mime that isn't silent,
as a shop without its stock,
as a model with no catwalk.

You're as useless as a car without a motor,
as a school without a rota,
as a pencil with no lead,
as a corpse that isn't dead.

You're as rubbish as a guitar without its strings,
as a bird without its wings,
as a lock without any key,
as a party with no tea.

Constance Mandair (13)
St Bede's School, Redhill

Winter's Carol

The wind wanders south,
to where it only knows.
When the sun opens her mouth
and people change their clothes.
The cold trapped in rotten cages,
runs rampant once more.
The angel of death rampages,
the purpose of summer ending its tour.

When the empty laughs and smiles of old joy,
run upon the wind a wild young boy.
The coming of cold presents new malice,
the new dark spawning minions from its chalice.
The leaves all but deceased their listening ears burnt dust,
a season of emptiness given birth by its crust.

Trees twisted and bent by the weather,
grass rusted and turned to ice.
Campaigning birds dare not drop a feather.
Cold, lost creatures stranded and tired,
frozen fish locked in time.
Winds return vengeful and angry,
the cold ever bitter long from fine.

Ryan Heartfield (13)
Selsdon High School

Trees And Trees

Spindly trees
sway precariously,
fallen trees
flatten the
undergrowth,
twisted,
mangled trees
wind around each other,
yellow marked trees
are on Death Row.

An aircraft drones
overhead.

I smell the
forest from
my notebook.

Lauren Cooke (15)
Selsdon High School

Life Is A Boat Upon The Sea

Life is a boat upon the sea,
Sometimes in storm, sometimes in ease.

You only get a push off
But then it's for you to choose.

There comes forks in the road,
As you move away.

One taking you somewhere,
While others else.

Sameera Ali (12)
Sutton High School

A Soldier's Battle In The Past, Present And Future

The misty skies from up above call upon the day,
Clouds sweep the eternity of blue but the shower of red still hurts,
The night before the first hour of rise an event so deadening
                                                took its place,
The deaths seemed like a nightmare but to someone a life of pain.

Every time his movement brings him on land he recalls the
                                first step he took on the scene,
Flashes back to that moment, that hour, that minute, that
                                second, where life changed for him,
The memories bring forth the idea of mind-forged manacles,
He wishes to unload the burden of remembering, of
                                knowledge, maybe even life,

He sees that day clearly and lives it and will die with it,
The soldier had stepped forward in the jaws of agony and blind hate,
Now when he walks with an umbrella by his side, he feels
                                the weapon he held that very day,
It's starting to rain and the coldness showers his broad,
                                aged shoulders just like that pastime,

The old man can't bear the drips of the gods and so takes
                                his umbrella out,
The soldier took out his gun poised at many of the Lord's creations,
Whish! goes the object at the sky which protects him from the rain,
Bang! went the object at the souls which protected him from
                                death but also a life of peace,

Life stopped at its clutches that very moment,
A hundred lifetimes stood and cried - for the men had gone,
The old man and the young soldier fell to the ground and wept,
Sixty-year-old tears have wept down that piteous cheek,
The chambers of his ancient heart unfold with grief.

His mind, like life dripping slowly from a soulless body is
                                           painted with regret,
As a young soldier, the fangs of regret and darkness bit
                                           him a thousand times,
As an old man, the fangs of woe have blunted yet
                                           strike a deep wound,
His heart aches for a morsel of forgiveness,
A grasp of peace,
But no solitude, no more solitude

This is his past, this is his present,
He prays it will not be his future.

Melanie Ranaweera (14)
Sutton High School

I Am Black!

I'm black
Some people seem to have a problem with that
I'm black
Some people seem unable to ignore that fact

Colour doesn't matter and
Coloured people's dreams shouldn't be shattered
Because of their skin
Others should be able to see within
The outer shell
That is how they may tell
That person's true identity
And experience their genuine personality

God created me black
And I'm truly proud of that
I do not lack anything
That any non-black has

I'm black . . . get over that!

Lizzi Yentumi (11)
Sutton High School

The Final Year

Biting wind,
Harsh cold air,
Frosted windows,
She sits in her chair.

Ice on streets,
Rain on roofs,
Noses red,
Winter is here.

Fresh morning sun,
Glistening dew in grass,
Fresh green plants,
She stares and lets it pass.

Children call across the street,
Leaves dangling from the trees,
Clear blue sky wrapped around the Earth,
Summer is here.

The air is much colder,
Nights are much longer,
Kids back at school,
Her pain's getting stronger.

Crunch red leaves
Beneath their feet,
Brown naked trees
Autumn has reached.

Biting wind,
Harsh cold air,
Frosted windows,
She is not there.

Niamh Connaughton (12)
Sutton High School

Feelings Of My World

Trapped! Trapped in a small dark world,
Grey walls all around me,
Escaping soon,
Going to safety.

On my way to the bundle,
Carrying on southwards,
Always on southwards,
Discovering a new way of living.

Sailing towards Italy,
After that to Denmark,
Asking God for help,
Lost compass down a cliff.

Must save little girl,
As pretty as can be,
First time I smiled today,
Looking down at beautiful Maria.

Sophie Penwarden (11)
Sutton High School

I Walk In The Dark

I walk in the darkness,
I follow your steps,
I have no feelings but I'll always be with you,
I grow and grow,
I shrink and shrink,
I hide, I hide, but I know I'll never die,
When the light comes,
I become powerful,
When the lights fades,
I become weak,
If I could only move for myself,
Me - and my army . . .
Of shadows.

Carla Busso (12)
Sutton High School

The Journey Beginning

Daylight dims as orange colours of sunshine dance about,
As the breeze sweeps in from the sea, I shiver,
Looking back down the hill at the town,
I gather my possessions into a bundle.

Sweeping my eyes around the small cave, I walk away,
Over my makeshift bridge, a plank.
Lights continuing to glow as I begin a long trek,
My small bundle over my shoulder.

Leaves rustle and branches gently sway,
Leaving behind the shimmering brook.
The sparkling blue sea towards the horizon,
At dawn I stop, look for food and hide.

At daylight, I wake to a salty smell,
Looking in horror at the sea left behind at dusk.
Has my compass failed
Or have I walked around in circles?

Harriet Trefusis (12)
Sutton High School

Libraries

Libraries, where quiet people work,
Like accountants or boring clerks,
But that is all that you know,
Because in the dead of night they go,

To strange places far and wide,
Where amazing things like to hide,
Like elephants or kangaroos
Or anything you wish to choose.

So next time you walk in
To a library dark and dim,
Don't just walk out or look around,
Because amazing things can be found.

Laura McLean
Sutton High School

Where Once I Stood

I stand on a spot where long ago,
A battle raged and foe faced foe,
Where lads who knew only love
Were force-fed hate and pain and blood.

I tread on a place where a gun was raised
And a finger smoothed its bayonet-blade,
A young boy held it with poise and pride,
'For life, for love, for us!' he cried.

I kneel by a patch with a battered cross,
To signify a life once lost,
'My friend and hero' the inscription reads,
Scribbled by that boy; 'No more!' he pleads.

I gather poppies in my hand and fling them over the barren land,
For every man who paid the price, he shall live eternal life,
But not that boy, he has yet to be,
He has not been judged; for that boy was me.

Emma Rice (14)
Sutton High School

Trains

Trains are speedy, trains are fast.
Trains whizz past in a blast.
They go round from place to place,
But don't go nearly as far as space.

Trains are long but not very wide,
But can fit in people side by side.
Trains have carriages and a driver's part too
And stop at places like Waterloo.

Trains are fun, but can cause accidents too,
Beware, they can hurt people like me and you.
So the next time you go on a train,
Don't derail onto a country lane.

Alyce Hayes (12)
Sutton High School

Why?

By the bank a body lay,
The features now disfigured.
The mud swirling all around,
A letter made its way:

Why do you hate me so very much?
What did I ever do?
All you wanted was to hurt me,
To make life good for you.

It must make you feel content,
To see helplessness in my eyes.
You've driven all my friends away,
By spreading hurtful lies.

I wonder why you made life hell,
To see me plead in vain.
Couldn't you have been my friend
Instead of causing all this pain?

I cannot go on any longer,
That I truly said goodbye,
Because of you I felt so small,
All this time I've lived a lie.

I tried to stand up to your taunts,
To show that I was brave.
You laughed at me and stole all hope,
To make me feel ashamed.

Alone and lost you made me feel,
Believing what you said.
You mocked until I'd lost myself,
In wishing I were dead.

Your childish games won't trouble me,
I feel pity at your fate,
Your insults, hits and jeering chants,
Will come to me too late.

Saman Zaman & Helen Sumping (14)
Sutton High School

My Room

My room is the place,
Where there's a lot of space,
For me to do what I like,
No one disturbs me, not even my daddy, Big Mike.

It's my secret space,
Where I can eat a fizzy lace.
My sisters can't annoy me,
So I can do everything in privacy.

It's wonderful and cosy,
Where my sisters can't be nosy.
I can eat and drink
And do a bit of a think.

My room is the place,
Where there's a lot of space,
For me to do what I like,
No one disturbs me, not even my daddy, Big Mike.

Faizah Ahmed (12)
Sutton High School

Life

As I drift through this world,
Facing whatever challenges it brings.
I'm forever changing,
Moving from stage to stage.

As I grow older, I leave people behind,
I walk alone with my thoughts accompanying me.
I meet new people,
I learn new things.

I don't know what this life will bring,
It is up to me to make something happen.
I have one chance to do it right,
This is it, my life.

Sana Sheikh (12)
Sutton High School

Life

You start off as hardly anything at all,
In your mother's womb, a small pink ball.
Then you start to grow and grow,
Your mum gets bigger, people know.

You are born! This is where life really starts,
With a small pink body and a beating heart.
A brand new name, maybe two,
Your parents are so proud of you.

You grow again, more and more,
You understand and learn with awe.
You learn to walk, you learn to talk,
You learn to play and use a fork.

Childhood flies and teens do too,
Times when you're good, times when you're blue.
Take lots of exams while working through school,
Learn to do sports and swim in a pool.

University, after that you're an adult,
Fall in love and secure the bolt.
Get a proper job; there's money to earn,
Have some children; bring more life to Earth.

Carry on with your life, get older and older,
Through the four seasons, warmer then colder.
As the years pass you dread the end,
When you will have to turn that very last bend.

That day has come, you fall asleep,
Never again will your heart ever beat.
But do not worry, do not fear,
Your life will start again another year.

Grace Lavelli (12)
Sutton High School

Friends

A friend is like a tree,
It starts off as a small seed
And grows and grows.

A friend is like a light bulb,
Sometimes on and sometimes off.

A friend is like a book,
A good source of information.

A friend is like a joke,
It makes you laugh.

A friend is like a window,
It helps you see through things.

A friend is like a knife,
It stabs you in the back
When you least expect it!

Lucy Parter (12)
Sutton High School

A Tree Through Seasons

In winter the tree stands dark and bare,
Against the sky, it creaks loudly in the high winds
And a few brown leaves flutter slowly to the ground.

In spring new buds appear on the branches
And soon fresh green leaves sprout and grow quickly,
Birds are busy in the high branches of the tree, building their nests.

In summer the leaves are fresh,
Fruit and nuts continue to grow as children
Climb the tree and swing from its branches.

In autumn the leaves change from green to beautiful orange and reds,
While squirrels scurry endlessly back and forth with their nuts,
Soon the ground beneath the tree is carpeted with the
                              brightly coloured leaves.

Charlotte Howson (12)
Sutton High School

My Friend

You are my rock;
I lean on you in times of trouble.
You give me warmth,
When all I feel is coldness.
You give me love,
When those around do not seem to care.
You show me the way to go,
When otherwise I would be lost in darkness.
You make me laugh,
When I am feeling down and unhappy.
You hold me afloat,
When I nearly drown in the world's sorrows.
We share so many good times,
Yet I know if ever I need you, you will always be there.
You are my friend; I am yours.
No one can ever take away what we share.

Alice Kendle (13)
Sutton High School

Twins

My twin is my other half
We will never ever part
With me every night and day
She'll always stay in my heart

My twin is my other half
Whether younger or older
Through all good times and bad times
She'll always stay in my heart

My twin is my other half
Stay together forever
We'll stay forever as one
She'll always stay in my heart.

Esther Nicoll (13)
Sutton High School

Death

Lying here all alone, weeping as I try
To remember all the things I said to make those people cry.
Did I treat my life with care?
Have I lived up to my best
Or was my life, as they say,
'A total waste of breath'?

I have no family next to me,
No one to hold my hand,
I wish I had the time to spare,
To tell them just how much I care.

'Sorry' is the only word,
You can read it on my lips.
'Sorry' is the only word,
I love them all to bits.

I feel a tear fall down my cheek,
As I stop and stare,
The pain I feel, it hits my chest,
I am no longer there.

Natasha Ward (13)
Sutton High School

The Sea

Waves of translucent,
Emerald and blue,
Shimmering diamonds,
Strewn askew.
Speckled with sapphires,
Lined with pearls.
Serenity, rippling
In glistening furls.

Barira Gore (16)
Sutton High School

The Volcano

The ground began to shudder,
I was scared out of my wits.
The lava was flowing nearer and nearer,
I ran further away.

The lava came closer,
It was moving faster,
I was exhausted,
My legs were like jelly and my feet did not move.

I had a burning feeling -
Come over me.
The lava had reached me,
The ground trembled.

I screamed,
I was dying.
Volcanic rock was breaking away,
It rolled towards me.

I lay on the ground in agony,
There was no help near,
I was alone, all alone,
There was nothing to do to save myself,

I took my last breath.

Catherine Langley (12)
Sutton High School

The Other Side Of Silence

Traffic murmurs in the nearby distance,
Dew on the turf twinkles and glistens,
Night-time gradually creeping in
And with the sun goes the deafening din,
The silence settles like thick fog
And swallows up all thought,
Everlasting stillness,
That suddenly is wrought,
The hazy scene of night-time rises,
This is the other side of silence.

The soft whisperings of the wind,
The cries in the dark that nobody hears,
The world's own song that no one can sing,
The quiet that is left at the turning of the years,
So dense, so unclear,
This is the other side of silence.

Day dawns and through enhanced quiet,
Screams cut through the darkness,
Noises of murder, pain and violence,
Rivers of blood overflow,
Nowhere to live, nowhere to go,
Children wailing in the streets,
Beggars lying at my feet,
Bombshells dropping one by one,
No one has lost,
Yet no one has won,
I hear the roaring of police sirens,
This is the other side of silence.

Catherine Kilkenny (12)
Sutton High School

Pieces Of British Pattern

Where tartan skirts flutter in a gusty gale,
The Scots toot on their bagpipes with a jig and a hop.
The dark Loch Ness, does Nessie live there?
And Hadrian's Wall,
Snaking across the horizon, long and frail.
A bookmark - dividing two pages.

Now England, where unburned St Paul's dome,
Curves in the twilight over Big Ben's spire
And the Millennium Eye, overlooking the Thames,
Goes round and round, a symbol of the century,
Like the Globe Theatre, which has stood the ages,
Though once burnt down and ground to ash.

The Emerald Isle, where the harp sings on
And religion divides the land in two,
Little green leprechauns with shamrocks dance,
In little green coats and small green hats,
As men gamble heartily on the horse races,
Over a pint of beer and ale!

The Welsh and their daffodils,
Sing of King Arthur and round tables,
And gallant knights and red dragons.
Broken castles tower over coastlines, shadowing the sands.
While the coalmines stand in the valleys,
The sheep and cattle graze o'er the hillside.

Thus the pieces of Britain,
Where history weaves its story.
The lace of war and greatness,
Which spins the centuries.

Mina Ghosh (11)
Sutton High School

The Present

Late at night on Christmas Eve,
I ponder what is under the tree,
Dollies, chocolate, a train set for Tom,
A woolly jumper I got for Mum.

Then I hear footsteps coming
And my heart starts running.
My door opens - it's only Mum,
She walks over
And pulls up my cover.

'Now get off to sleep
And don't go and peep
At all the presents under the tree,
Wait till the morning,
I know it's quite boring -
But please try to sleep.'

I got up quickly
And awoke everyone else,
We all went downstairs
And looked under the tree -
A present that was addressed for me!

My heart was pounding,
I couldn't stop wondering,
Just what it could be.

The paper unravelled and sitting inside,
A book? A hat? A toy perhaps?
It was none of these things,
But a lovely necklace and a set of rings.

Emma Harkins (12)
Sutton High School

The Camp Life

Dark and rotten,
Cold and dreary,
Alone in a world,
Trapped with no escape.

No one would want to,
No one can come,
To this place where the only thing free,
Is the evil around me.

I have no point to live,
No one could bring safety,
To this place where I'm stuck,
Like an animal in a cage.

Out of here it would be a dream,
Yet I will never know,
For I am David
And this is the life I live.

Kyndra Vorster (11)
Sutton High School

Alone

The wind whispers through her barren heart,
From her love she has had to part.
All alone but for her pain,
She writhes and weeps and cries his name.
Inside it feels as though her soul has been torn,
But there is nothing she can do but cry and mourn,
The sunlight in her life has vanished,
All love and happiness cruelly banished
And at the dawn of every new day,
She desperately wishes her life away.
To end this torture is what she yearns most,
To join her love in the world of ghosts.
For living alone is not living at all
And so to the depths of despair she does fall.

Antonia Williams (14)
Sutton High School

What Am I?

A soul trapped in a body,
Which will not be let free.

A brain trapped in a soul,
Which is kept weeping inside of me.

A thought trapped in a mind,
To be locked up forever.

A heart that is craving to be loved,
Cornered into a vortex of sorrow.

A mind that is free to think,
A body without liberty to roam.

A pair of eyes no use to me,
Four grey walls and a wire mesh fence is all to see.

My being is meaningless to all,
My presence is puzzling.

What am I?

Krupa Thakker (11)
Sutton High School

My Mum

My mum is a star in the dark night sky,
My mum is a flame that will never ever die,
My mum is a breeze on a stormy sea,
My mum is the feeling that makes me, me.

My mum is a hope in a far-off land,
My mum is a drum in a big brass band,
My mum is the pin that holds me together,
I love my mum and I will forever!

Hannah Nicoll (13)
Sutton High School

Fire

Fire demons, fire demons,
Devil worshippers, fire demons,
Must save the little girl,
I owe it to God.

Little girl so quietly sleeping,
Bound to her chair,
One, two, the ropes are off,
I must do this for God.

Breathe,
Breathe,
We both are out,
I've done this for God.

Brown eyes,
So amazingly pretty,
The girl has awoken,
Thank you God.

House, house,
Scary house,
Never enter a house,
Help me God.

Jennifer Ferguson (11)
Sutton High School

The Chase

Running
Tripping
Stumbling
They know I'm here
And they're coming to get me

Lungs screaming
Head spinning
Nowhere to hide
They'll find me here
No one can hide from them

No escape
Have to stop
I lean against a tree
All the time they're closing in
Baying for my blood

I hear their barks
So close now
The end is near
There are here; they have won
They yelp and surround me

Intense pain
Blood everywhere
Slipping away
I hear the crack of bones and
The scrape of teeth on sinew.

Why me?

Helen Thorpe (14)
Sutton High School

Panda

I am a little baby panda,
Living in the lush forests green,
But I'm the only panda
Ever to be seen.

I've never seen another panda,
Wonder what they would look like?
But I'm the only panda,
What do I look like?

I roam through my forests,
Searching high and low.
Will I find a panda?
I really don't know.

I've been looking for ages and ages
And now I want a drink,
This is really outrageous,
I must sit down and think.

What's that over there?
It's drinking from my pool.
Well, it's not his fault,
He wants a drink too.

Wait, it's me,
Not him.
I'm the one in the pool,
How could I be such a fool?

I am what I am,
A baby panda.
This is what I look like,
Black and white.

But, am I a black panda with white spots
Or am I a white panda with black spots?

Nivedita Chakrabarti (13)
Sutton High School

My Life

I stand alone
Forever enclosed
No friend, no teacher
No parent or sibling
I have no future or pleasing past
My destiny is written

I sleep, I eat
I forever drink
Like an animal
Enclosed in a zoo
Locked up in a cage
With the key thrown away

I was never given a chance
To prove myself
Always being punished
Because of someone else
Their hatred's never-ending
Our turmoil everlasting

I dream tomorrow
Will bring joy and happiness
But every morning
There is no change
Hour turns into day
Will there ever be any change?

My life is hatred
My life is spite
My life has no love
My life has no kindness
My life is this, my life is that
There is no life inside this camp.

Sophia Kavanagh (11)
Sutton High School

Why?

Why is a desolate word,
Lonely and foreboding.
Why turns your heart to ice,
To an ironclad chamber of pain.
Why is cool as a cucumber,
Moving from place to place.
Why is the raindrop on the window
That runs like a tear on your cheek.
It drips down your spine
Making shivers like splintering glass.
The slapped cheek at a crowded party,
The child in front of your car,
Just a fraction too late to slow down.
Why is the word that you think of
When everyone knows you're alone.
Because you know that it's all your fault,
Why did I do it? Why didn't I stop?
Why, oh why?

Lucy Bidmade (15)
Sutton High School

Distance Is The Threat Of Life

It is distance that kills the heart.
It is worry that hurts the most.
Knowing my dad was so far away.
The only thoughts that came rushing through my mind
Were things that could cause death.
I never thought life could be so tough.
That one phone ring brought it all to life.
My dad had been beaten up by thieves,
That one call changed my life.
Should I blame all this on one horrifying call?
Distance is everyone's weakness.

Shaline Fazal (12)
Sutton High School

I Am David

Trapped, trapped in two worlds,
Their world and my world.
I let the days pass so freely,
Just thinking about the next meal.

The bitter wind whips through my heart,
Stinging like a wasp.
I shiver, I feel someone wrap a blanket round me,
I let it fall to the floor, they gave it to me.

I will break free someday,
I will get my revenge.
They have robbed me of my childhood,
I will never forgive them.

They do not rule me,
They never will,
I will not let them,
I am David and they cannot rob me of that.

Alice Heathfield (11)
Sutton High School

What Is This World?

What is this world?
Beautiful, picturesque,
God's creation,
Full of peaceful humanity.

What is this place?
Passionate, worshipping,
Appealing, desiring;
Packed with kinship and faith.

Why is *this* world?
Cruel, objectionable,
God's creation,
Changed, with humanity.

Why is this place?
With authority, seizure,
Conflict and massacre,
Packed with pain and hatred.

Charlotte Irvine (11)
Sutton High School

Prisoner In The Camp

What do I have to show for my life?
Four grey walls in a vortex of terror,
A violent guard where a parent should stand
And a mind confined to *their* way of thinking.

Questions like targets that I can't reach,
Will I ever know the answers?
So I lie here - sedated into routine,
While *they* laugh and sneer.

I am a young boy with the past of a man,
My mind knows too much,
My eyes have seen rituals of evil,
Performed by *them.*

We are never alone,
Like vultures - they watch us,
We cannot escape the hungry desire,
Of *them* - the camp guards.

Sarah Daoud (11)
Sutton High School

Maybe . . .

Maybe the world known as wonderful,
The world is beautiful, but at the inside they don't know
What's going to be.

Maybe there is dirt inside,
But maybe there is clean inside,
Nobody knows what's going to be.

The flowers will rise again,
But they died soon as possible,
Maybe they will rise again as they did.

Maybe the world is going to get darker,
No lightness or brightness,
But maybe there is a hope, that people believe.

Cries, shout, kill, mistake,
These make us terrified and be horrible,
But maybe,
Kind, brightness and happy smiles,
These will change us
And it is a hope which is wanted.

In-Young Choi (13)
Sutton High School

Darkened Memories

My mind creeps back and sees the shadowed figure
And I fall into the inky blackness all over again,
The icy wind pushes me downwards,
To the darkness, the terrible darkness.

I creep back to my childhood,
Dissolve once more through the wall of dimension,
Falling further and further and further,
To the darkness, the terrible darkness.

The wind howls and the rain beats hard,
But deep, deep down the blackness is suffocating,
Swallowing me down through the nothingness,
To the darkness, the terrible darkness.

I ascend the rusting staircase,
The dark, thick and humid around me,
I open the door where death is waiting,
In the darkness, the end of the darkness.

Nancy Godden (12)
Sutton High School

Hallowe'en

Witches scream
And devils cackle,
Ghosts fly,
While phantoms tackle.

Lights turn off
And fires burn,
There are bloodsucking moths
And cobweb walls turn.

Evil eyes stare, watching,
As tombstones come alive,
There are wild traps for catching,
While poltergeists swoop and dive.

The grandfather clock strikes midnight,
As the phantom organ plays,
The haunted house is such a sight,
It will haunt you in all your days!

Pleasant dreams . . .

Laura Hamer (12)
Sutton High School

True Face Of Our World

Can we make the past come back to us?
Can we love each other?
Can we be friends, not enemies?
Why, why do we need to hate each other?

The world will make mistakes today,
The world will kill each other today,
The world will be enemies forever,
Please, please, why can't we be friends?

The war isn't over, it's just started.

Things will happen again and again,
People won't realise what 'peace' means forever.
No one in the whole world will know
What 'peace' means.

They made the biggest mistake of their lives
But they didn't realise.

One day, one day they will realise their mistake
But it will be too late.

Hayoon Lee (12)
Sutton High School

Try And Guess What This Sonnet Is About

The movement graduates as time passes
Sense of humanity becomes like a rope
The meaning of life gives us all chances
As for every being life brings hope

For young and old chances can bring changes
And time will continue to proceed on
But dealing comes in different ranges
Some choose odd ways; some will carry a tonne

Some see their lives as a complete waste
When something happens which is very tragic
They need to explore to different taste
You can't take time waiting for something magic

Live life going through a rainforest
And accept the change whilst being modest

A poem about growing up.

Zara Syed (13)
Sutton High School

The Deep Blue Yonder

A home for many
where dreams alight
in the deep blue yonder

The lapping waves
and shells of coral
in the deep blue yonder

The freeness and smoothness
as you glide along
the deep blue yonder

The sparkle of the water
like diamonds and pearls
embraces you with love
in the deep blue yonder.

Sabrina Marsh (12)
Sutton High School

What

What is life?
Simply just pain and strife.
What brings us happiness and joy?
Life is like an alluring, seductive and captivating flower,
One starts off small and elusive,
Then begins to grow and bloom.
Bees allow them to disseminate themselves,
Finally due to some or other cause,
The flower begins to wilt or is picked
And life is simply snatched away from it.

What are we?
Just toys in the eye of the creator?
Perhaps we serve no purpose at all
And are simply destroyers of our beautiful Earth.
We are all interlinked,
Everyone's lives revolving around one another.
We may even all be related.
Is that possible?
Each one of us individuals and unique
And yet we are so similar.

What is going to happen to us?
Will we die?
Perhaps we do not even exist.
Will we go to Heaven or Hell?
The good go to Heaven and the bad to Hell,
However how can we define good and bad people?
Who has the right to say that we are bad?
Conceivably, our bodies may simply decompose in the
                                        aloof, solitary Earth
Or maybe we are reincarnated,
We could be ants or even rhinos in our future lives.
Therefore the question arises,
What are we in the whole scale of the universe?

Alina Fazal (15)
Sutton High School

Whispers And Shadows

Gentle whispers,
Tickling my ear.
The soft warmth of breath,
Softly . . . softly . . .
Reaching out,
Almost touching,
So close and yet so far,
Sounds, almost audible,
But not quite.
You strain yourself,
Trying to understand,
They darken your heart,
Entering your very soul.
A presence barely there
And yet so close you feel like crying.
But they are just shadows,
That melt in the sunlight,
Gone, fading to nothing,
So soon you aren't even sure they were there.
You are wary,
You want them gone,
You think they have flown
Away on the wind,
But they return,
Taking you again to the darkness,
Swallowing your life,
Your friends, your family,
Until you sit alone in the dark.
Utterly, completely alone,
Except for the whispers and shadows.

Emma McLean (14)
Sutton High School

If Only

If only I had told her what she had meant to me,
Then maybe she would still be here
Standing next to me.

If only I had rung her up to say a simple hi,
Her phone would now be answered
So I could say my last goodbye.

If only I had saved a seat so we could sit together,
I wouldn't be sitting here alone,
Time going on forever.

If only I had called her back when she had walked away,
I could have given her a hug,
Which may have made her stay.

If only I had talked to her to see how she was feeling,
I could have helped her instead of seeing
Her hanging from the ceiling.

If only I had treated her in that special way,
She may have realised how much she's loved
And how she's missed today.

I feel so bad now that she's gone,
The person to blame is I.
I feel I should have done much more,
So she wouldn't have wanted to die.

Maybe I could have helped her through,
Maybe she wouldn't have lied
And told me that she felt OK,
Before going to commit suicide.

Katie Madden (15)
Sutton High School

A Creator's Disaster

In the beginning, there was a Creator,
Yes, indeed, there was one,
He looked at nothing - decided on something
And soon it was very much done.

Life, it seemed, was a wonderful thing,
Yes, don't take for granted, this living,
People didn't care why they were there,
Just as long as . . . they were there and very much with it.

But then came the disaster,
And nobody seemed to care,
As death, hate and greed paid a visit,
Except the Creator, who watched in despair.

As the corrupted ones went,
To Hell or to Heaven, to which they preferred,
They were asked: 'Who to blame?'
And to the Creator it was referred.

Love couldn't save them
And in doing what they thought was right,
They snatched away the Creator's gift,
By involving the innocent in an unnecessary fight.

You can ask, 'Where is the love?'
And what war is good for
But the answer we will find
Inside ourselves is: 'What are *we* good for?'

Se-yi Hong (14)
Sutton High School

Georgina And The Dragon

Once in a far-off land, the dragon roamed free,
He ate the people one by one and giggled with glee.
Each day there was terror, as the lots were drawn out,
The loser was eaten, none heard their shout.

One day Princess Georgina pulled out the shortest straw,
The king and queen were most upset, they said, 'He'll eat her raw!'
But Georgie was brave and off she marched, her dress trailing behind,
Wearing high-heeled shoes, a diamond brooch and every jewel she
could find.

The dragon was waiting, he looked up and smiled, this evening's
dinner had come,
But Georgie stood bold, her handbag held tight, the battle had hardly
begun.

Out kicked her heels, on the dragon's scaly back,
The force was so hard, he fell with a *smack!*
The dragon was irate, he set her dress ablaze,
She screamed, 'You brute! That dress was all the craze!'

The dragon's tail lashed out across the dirty floor,
But Georgie was now ready and knew there would be more.
She whipped out her mascara and poked him in the eye,
The dragon grunted once and spread his wings to fly.

But Georgie was on top again and wouldn't let him go,
She tied a necklace to his tail and held on from below.
She yanked him to the ground again and made her last approach,
This time upon his forehead with her diamond brooch.

The dragon now collapsed and lay down to die,
Georgie roared, 'Whoopee! Wahoo!' There was no reply.
She took out her hairbrush and poked it in his side,
He made no move at all, he had definitely died.

So next time there's a dragon, giggling with glee,
Remember Princess Georgina who fought to victory.
She used what she had with her to fight the ugly beast,
Then went back home to celebrate, with a great big feast.

Helen Stewart (13)
Sutton High School

A Homeless Girl

She woke up from that devouring sleep
Such a powerful time of dreaming
She knows she must move on today
Yet her eyes flicker, disbelieving

Searching around her she takes in the view
Just brick walls and freezing grey pavements
Tonight she wanted some quiet seclusion
Instead of this stone-cold enslavement

She shifts through the street amongst dirty looks
Frowned upon for the clothes she is wearing
Tears spill from her eyes - though quickly disguised
She detests all the flavourless staring

She finds an area of flourishing foliage
She'll settle for this tonight
More serene is this place, among views of the moon
And silvery, soft, dappled light

She looked at the stars and huddled her knees
Wondering if the stars were hearing
She glanced around at the leaves on the ground
And started to make out a clearing

Falling down on her space she looked at the place
A different one from this morning
Warming herself as well as she could
She could not stop herself yawning

Back to her fantasy of castles and clouds
Of princes and young, handsome men
Finally she found her one true home
That devouring sleep once again.

Priya Floyd (14)
Sutton High School

Winter's Day

You were the sun
And I the cold moon.
I was so very alone that day,
That winter's afternoon.
All the things that I had longed to mention,
I never had the chance to say,
The thoughts I had of you were forever lost,
Abandoned in the heart of the crystal depths
Of that winter's frost.
I tell myself that it must have been fate,
That ripped you away from my life,
But still I know I was that moment too late.
Oh how I am still able to recall,
How you slipped through my fingers
And I allowed you to fall.
Someday now we may be together again.
Today, however, I know it cannot be as such.
It seems like it has been this way for eternity, my dear.
Never can I feel your warm touch.
To have spoken of our love,
Was to have spoken of our doom.
So now we stand apart from one another,
You hidden from me by a wall of gloom.
Now, all I feel is an aching void within
And so I wait alone and pray.
Reminded by others that I long for a sin,
Ever hoping for that winter's day.

Anne Higgins (14)
Sutton High School

Night Traffic

You roar at me, defiantly.
The glass earmuffs will barely absorb what you shout.
You are the heavy breathed wind;
The laboured breaths of an asthmatic old man.
Your dialect can't be placed, the language can't be read,
But you're explaining something to me.
Light buzzing bees race through you, loaded slow movers learn you.
For a few moments you let the silence cross over you
And then the warning lights of impending noise alert us, silently.
Choreographed lights define equality, markings of red, yellow and
white denote power and statues of fluorescent paint are
                                    warnings of treacherous turns.
You have touched each sense of mine and yet I cannot
                            comprehend what it all might mean.
You can explain to me every night in the same deep monotone
With the same bland words, but you can't make me
                            understand your way of life.

And so we exist, side by side in the same world,
Knowing of but not knowing why.

I think that saddens me.

Rachel Cooper (17)
Sutton High School

A Pirate's Song

The crested waves lap the shores of death,
Their hearts of gold are put to rest,
The murderous skies will silence the night,
When blackened souls sing and captains take flight.
For the world before is hidden with treasure,
An abundance of bounty for buccaneer's pleasure,
The cannons will fire and blood will be shed,
Swords will be drawn and Silver is dead.
For the kingdom of bones beckons you in,
When the twilight of rum is surrounded by sin,
'Shiver me timbers,' one man cries,
Spaniards are captured, another man dies.
The laden ships sail for the leagues of tomorrow,
As barrels of wealth are dripping in sorrow.
A howl is heard from the ship's tallest peak,
The crow's nest is sounded but still the cabin sleeps.
An island is calling for the Devil's return,
A bloodstained dawn was unleashed and burned.

Helen McEwan (14)
Sutton High School

The Eliminator

He comes, he comes, who is he?
Or perhaps, you don't know, it might be a she.
Stealing stealthily down the hall,
Getting bigger all the time, but definitely not small.
Now, you can see it clearly!
He jumps and nearly,
Got you.
But who?
Who could it be?
The thing it has looks like a bee,
But I have seen it before . . .
It wipes out people by the score!
The dreaded Eliminator!
Eliminator . . .
Eliminator . . .
I'm a-gonner.

Danielle Grayston (12)
Sutton High School

The Emperor Penguin

I have jet-black skin and a belly of snowish-white,
I swim in arctic waters all day
And have forty winks at night,
Fish look upon me
As a daunting, terrifying predator,
But humans look upon me
As a cute and coquettish creature,
However I am the emperor penguin
And live on the coldest place on Earth,
In between the lumpy snow is where I like to lurk,
My wings are flippers and my feet are webbed,
The snow and sleet are my silken bed
And tobogganing down slopes with my mighty head
Is what I mostly like to do,
So next time join me in the snow,
For penguins are the best you know,
Now you are all my special friends
And now this poem is at its end.

Darshikah Gnanakumar (12)
Sutton High School

Alone

When I lie in bed at night,
I just think of your delight.
To see me laying there alone,
My sister out of sight.

I just wish she'd come back,
Come back down to Earth.
But no, she's in Heaven,
All because of your birth.

When you ran her over that day,
I looked and saw her lay.
She showed no emotion or movement of her body
And all you could do was run away.

You don't know what you did to our lives,
Ruined, shattered, it was out of the blue.
I just with you'd give yourself up,
So the police would know it was you.

Jessica Sumping (12)
Sutton High School

I Am David

I'm trapped inside this gloomy, dark place,
I feel so unloved, with a broken heart and upset soul,
Enclosed by the walls of dull grey colours,
My fear of things grows larger as the time goes on,
I am David, scared and alone.

I need to escape from this horrid camp,
There is nothing to do and no one to see,
My heart thumps on like a ticking clock,
When I will have the chance to go . . . I don't know,
I am David, looking ahead to the future.

I wonder what it will look like outside?
Who will be there? Will they care or will they just stare?
I do not know what I should do, I do not know what will happen,
Maybe it will be no better, maybe it will be beautiful,
I am David and I don't know what to expect.

Catherine Branter (11)
Sutton High School

Winter!

I'm staring out of the window,
On a misty winter's day.
Snow falls gently to the ground,
Forming a blanket of white.

Snowmen sit by the hillside,
As they pass the day away.
The children stand beside them,
Admiring what they have made.

Snowballs soar through the sky,
As children fight with their friends.
Sometimes they hit the windows,
But mostly they hit the ground.

I'm staring out of the window,
On a misty winter's day.
Snow falls gently to the ground,
Forming a blanket of white.

Kathryn Griffiths (13)
Sutton High School

Spring

Spring is when the daffodils start to peep out of
The fresh green grass,
When new, fluffy, baby lambs struggle to walk
Among the glimmering field,
When the bright, shining sun shines down on us,
Spring.

In spring the swift blow of wind passes us,
The soft shower of rain scatters upon the earth,
New colourful flowers blossom on the trees,
Spring.

In spring juicy berries start to grow,
Butterflies flutter about shining in the sunshine,
The birds sing a beautiful, warm tune as they
Admire the view.
Spring.

Wajeeha Ahmed (12)
Sutton High School

I'm Leaving

As I now stand alone in the world once more
I feel so sad and upset
I shall never be the same again

The first time I looked into her eyes
I knew I would love this girl always
I am now in deep despair whenever I think of her
I am carefree apart from my secret heartache

I am sure she will live a beautiful life
Without me
She will remember me
I hope

I will always remember her
Lips the tenderest of crimsons
Eyes the deepest of browns
And her delicate doll face

Her pretty face looking down on me
Even though my strange eyes glare
Even though I am a camp boy
I am David. No one can change that.

Hannah Tiernan (11)
Sutton High School

Green And Silver Murky Hills

Walking silently I shiver,
My hands are blue and numb,
I cough a rusty cough,
But still I walk on,
Through the green and silver murky hills.

The frost on my shoes,
The ice on the pond,
I feel as though I am going to die,
But still I walk on,
Through the green and silver murky hills.

More and more tired I grow,
Feeling dizzy I carry on,
But then I fall,
I fall helplessly,
Down into the green and silver murky hills.

I am lying weakly on the hills
And slowly I push myself up,
It's no good, I feel my hands and feet no more,
So there I am dying, this is the end,
Now I'm dead, I died in the green and silver murky hills.

Alexandra San Miguel-Brathwaite (12)
Sutton High School

The Four Seasons

Winter - cold, windy and a lot of rain,
The bare trees,
Sway from side to side,
The flowers are dead,
The fields of green, turn bare
And all the animals disappear.

The flowers grow back, spring is here,
The colour comes back to life,
The trees start turning green,
The animals show their faces again,
Cold breeze is still there,
Now the people are waiting for summer.

Finally, the summer is here,
The scorching hot weather,
Everyone packs for the summer holidays,
The world is bright again,
Children playing in the park,
With smiles on their faces.

The autumn is here,
When the children play in the leaves,
The leaves turn to bright colours,
The leaves start to fall, floating in the air,
Everyone back to school,
These are the four seasons!

Priyanka Amin (1)
Sutton High School

Wolf

As fast as lightning
As steady as a rock
As strong as a raging fire
As mysterious as the dark side of the moon

Yellow bombs
A staring child
A man outside
His eyes are wild

A mirror room
A moon-gazer van
A note on the windscreen
From the wild-eyed man

'Who's afraid of the big bad wolf?'
Screaming, screaming, running
Danger, danger, get there quick
Heart frantically pumping

All are safe in the warm brick house
The wolf has turned and gone
Rest and sleep, for now at least
This battle you have won!

Rachel Elgy (12)
The Warwick School

Wolf

He stalks me quietly through the night,
I walk on - his unsuspecting prey.
His wide, golden eyes have perfect sight,
But only on me they stay.

Not a rock, nor a boulder stands in his way,
With his paws so careful and quick.
A grin crosses his face as he begins to bay
And his tongue lolls out with a flick.

His paws are rising,
At last he is truly free.
I should be in hiding,
But he's gained on me.

There's no way out,
He knows this too.
It's too late to shout,
My eyes, how they grew.

A long grey muzzle
And burning amber eyes.
His teeth sharp as daggers,
But the wolf I see is - inside!

Leonie Figov (12)
The Warwick School

Wolf Poem

The wolf creeps slowly along to the door,
His feet patter along the cold concrete floor.
His sharp claws tap on the wood
And then he pulls up his big black hood.
He looks through the glass for Nan to come quick,
She creaks the door open and leans on her stick.
He runs in, closing the door,
Nan beckons him in further and leans her stick against the wall.
The lightning starts again outside,
Cassie comes in, the wolf hides.
She asks Nan why the door is shut,
But her nan soon says, 'Don't interrupt.'
Cassie goes back and falls asleep,
Until the morning when her alarm clock goes beep!
Nan comes in with the suitcase, brown,
Cassie looks up and gives a frown.
She wonders why she is going this time,
Nan looks at her like everything's fine.
Cassie sees the door shut across the hall,
It needs to air, who is there?
Cassie hugs Nan and sets off,
Wondering where her mum will be living this time!

Rhiannon Barber (12)
The Warwick School

Animals

Animals, animals are so cute,
they look nice when they're wearing a suit.

I like the way that rabbits hop.
they would be nice in a frilly top.

Rabbits, rabbits are my best,
I like birds when they are in pretty nests.

I don't like animals feeling so sad,
because it makes me really mad.

Sammy Matheson (11)
The Warwick School

Wolf

The wolf creeps slowly, descending the cellar.
His feet go pitter-patter on the hard stone floor.
His unsuspecting prey waits alone on her bed.
Towering over her ready to strike,
Nan comes to rescue the wolf from doing wrong.
The wolf turns and sees Nan's stick raised above her head,
He cowers away from Nan's piercing stare.
She steps towards the cowering wolf to stand by Cassie.
Befriending the wolf each word she says,
Moving forever closer towards the wolf.
Telling the wolf don't move or she'll do something she won't regret.
The wolf feels something he's never felt before,
He feels it really bad, he thinks it may be fear.
Nan senses his feelings and thinks to take advantage,
She steps towards the wolf and pokes it with her stick.
Out the end comes a shiny silver bullet,
The wolf before her eyes becomes a human, a human named Lyall.

Jennifer Austin (12)
The Warwick School

Sweets

Chocolate is delicious,
I like it oozing in my mouth,
I like it when I melt it so it's all soft,
I like it when I put it in the fridge so that it goes all hard,
When I break the chocolate
I like the sound of it cracking.

Rhubarb and custard sweets are hard and colourful,
I like the taste when I suck them,
They get smaller and smaller the harder I suck,
When they have gone, I think *should I have another one?*

Katie Miller (12)
The Warwick School

Sam The Man

There once was a man called Sam,
He lived in a house which was glam,
Every night and every day,
He'd make a wish and say,
'What a lucky man I am.'

Sam was a man with a cornet,
If you were there you would have seen it,
From the day of his birth,
When he landed onto Earth,
You would have thought that he'd actually drawn it.

Now you have heard of Sam the man,
But I didn't tell you he drives in a van,
From pencil to lead,
He is now dead,
But he still has his dark brown tan.

Francesca Bragg (11)
The Warwick School

Wolf

There is a wolf in you and I,
It is an angry wolf around mess,
It is an angry wolf around Dad,
It is a misunderstanding wolf when it gets told to go,
It is a misunderstanding wolf around Mum,
It is a confused wolf around yellow plastic,
It is a confused wolf when it is around Lyall,
It is a kind wolf around Nan,
It is a kind wolf around strangers,
It is a scared wolf around a squat,
It is a scared wolf when it gets told 'Wolf'
This wolf can be a caring, loving wolf
Eager to teach its cubs,
It can be a screaming wolf around other wolves
But also it is a sensible, understanding wolf that loves others.

Amelia Guare (12)
The Warwick School

Poverty

When the sun did rise,
Out came some black flies,
Disease is spreading,
They don't have bedding,
The people do die,
No money to buy,
People are starving,
But still doesn't stop.

Here we have used them,
Even have whipped them,
Many years ago,
Have no toys to throw,
Living in a shack,
When the sky turns black,
Nothing to give light,
But still doesn't stop.

Anastasia Celesius (13)
The Winston Churchill School

I Am An Ant

I am a little ant,
I really am quite small,
I crawl around all day and night,
Life is just a ball.

I play with all my ant friends,
I'm having lots of fun,
My feet are now all sticky,
I've just stepped in some gum.

I'm walking along the street now,
I'm hearing the cars hoot,
It's getting very scary,
Oh no, a great big *fooooot* . . .

. . . *Squash*.

Cassie John (13)
The Winston Churchill School

Losing You

I sit on the sill and watch snowflakes fall,
The sky has turned from blue to grey,
I sit there on the floor and think,
Behind me the red sunset begins to sink.

My world has been ripped apart
And hope has been taken from my soul,
I feel like nothing; an empty body,
With a heart as black as coal.

I step down from the window,
I can't bear the sudden thought,
That I'll lose what's behind that big closed door,
Laying quietly the baby that I adore.

The child, my child, lies and watches me,
Torments my very mind,
Her tiny hands and tiny toes,
Brings tears to trickle down my nose.

I peer into the room that I have come to dread,
I see her lying fast asleep in her tiny bed,
There's no sound in the room apart from the sucking of her teat
And the faint sound of her tiny heartbeat.

Her pale pink dress makes her seem so fair,
That I can't help but smile at her blonde curly hair,
Her mouth starts to open and her eyes start to cringe,
As she slowly yawns and pushes away her fringe.

So I'll kiss her little cheeks
And stare into her eyes,
My dear child, my sweet child,
I'm letting you go to live a happier life than mine.

Claudia Foxcroft (13)
The Winston Churchill School

From Love To Hate

She spent more and more time away,
He didn't know what was wrong.
She was out almost every day
And she was out for far too long.

He started to ask the people around him
Where exactly it was she goes,
Someone said, 'I know where she is.'
'At last someone who knows.'

He quickly rushed over to see her,
Without even thinking ahead.
He stopped for a minute
And to himself he said,

'We were happy together,
Or so I thought,
I thought our love would last forever.'
But then they were caught.

He saw her with his best friend
And they weren't just talking.
Their love had come to an abrupt end,
Cos this boy, he was walking.

She shouted for him to turn around,
But he got out his gun,
He shot and then he hit the ground,
The girl she did run.

She ran and ran until she reached him,
But it was too late.
She was crying, she was screeching,
Their love had grown to hate.

Debbie Gee (13)
The Winston Churchill School

The Ballad Of The Titanic

The Titanic, a floating palace,
One of the safest ships of its time
Set sail from Southampton harbour,
A White Star Liner in its prime.

A legend before even leaving,
With no expenses having been spared,
Carrying the rich and immigrants
To their fate, they were unprepared

Four days into her maiden voyage,
On a clear, dark, moonless sky night,
Tragedy struck her and those on board,
As a huge iceberg came into sight.

The captain was starting to worry,
He knew that the ship was too large.
Too heavy to turn and miss the iceberg,
Too fast to slow down and take charge.

Black, icy water soon filled the bow
And the ship could take no more strain,
As slowly its stern rose into the air,
Those below only watching with pain.

The dark ocean was slowly opening,
The Titanic was being sucked inside.
A legend before even leaving,
A bigger legend under the tide.

Very few people were alive then
And only know of the stories told,
But for those involved in the tragedy,
It seems like yesterday, true and bold.

Karin Ferris (13)
The Winston Churchill School

Santa Doesn't Wear Black

'Santa don't exist,' they said.
'Now shut your mouth and go to bed.'
I knew I was right when I said they were wrong
Cos Santa's as real as the day is long.

They sent me to bed and turned off the light
And left me to ponder into the night.
But soon I heard muffled footsteps on the roof
And I was certain that was a reindeer's hoof.

I jumped out of bed and ran down the stairs
And glanced at the fireplace, tingling in my hairs.
A fat man in black clothes tumbled into the room
And I thought . . . *that must be Santa . . . if not, then whom?*

In his hands the man held a gun and a bag
And on the bag was written in big letters *swag*.
He cocked the gun and aimed it right at my head
And said, 'Don't move, kid, or I'll render you dead.'

I told him, 'Santa, you're feeling grumpy today.'
He said, 'Not another step, or I'll make you pay.'
Then I told him that for Christmas I wanted a pony
And a zombie outfit, so I can scare my friend, Tony.

Then with a splintering crash a man burst in,
A fat man in red, with a funny hat thing.
He had a shotgun and a dozen grenades
And strapped to his arms were wolverine blades.

'Ho, ho, ho, Merry Christmas!' he said
And with one fatal shot blew off the guy's head.
Then he turned around and walked back through the door
And the legend of Santa was a legend no more.

Andrey Barsky (13)
The Winston Churchill School

My New PC

I bought a PC yesterday,
From a shop down Buyers Road.
I struggled on for half an hour,
Carrying my heavy load.

I plugged it in and turned it on,
I watched it come to life.
I'd no idea that it would be,
The source of all my strife.

I wanted to do a simple thing,
Type a letter for Philip, my mate.
I typed it out but it would not print,
I was starting to get slightly irate.

I tried to surf the Internet
And read any e-mail I had.
My inbox was filled with junk mail,
I was starting to get *really* mad.

I played the latest arcade game,
'Space Attack - The Alien Fight',
The baddie beat me in ten seconds flat,
I was starting to get *very* uptight.

It had made me get so annoyed,
I smashed my shoe through the screen.
I threw the machine out the window,
I *truly* was venting my spleen.

Steven John (13)
The Winston Churchill School

The Twin Towers

Bin Laden had been planning
The terrorists were on the plane
With guns and knives at the ready
They all must be insane

The terrorists knew it was their time
They gave the passengers grief
They tied up both pilots
There were screams of disbelief

The Twin Towers were in sight
The plane was hurtling through the sky
On the phone to loved ones
All the passengers could do was cry

The plane was aimed
There was a shattering sound
All the glass was cracking
Some poor souls will never be found

No one considered there would be another plane
Suddenly there was another crack
But for the passengers on board
There was no turning back

The rescuers started streaming
Just trying to do their job
The carnage they encountered
Brought on many a sad sob

Relatives will never again
Hear their loved ones on the phone
But at least they can always remember
They will never mourn alone.

Michelle Taylor (13)
The Winston Churchill School

The Middle Passage

As I write this poem
The shackles rub my wrists
Red raw ruby wrists
For all the world to see

I cannot read this page for tears
They mix with blood and sweat
Children, mothers, brothers, fathers
Are dying all around

Bound together, tied together
Lying on the ground
Naked . . . stripped of clothes
Possessions and dignity

Why did it happen to us?
We hurt no one
We shamed no one
We provoked no one

We have our religions
Our ways and traditions
We have our towns and village
Our Heaven and our Hell

How different are we to you?
You rape our women
Kill our children
Drown our people's ways

We are bound now
To a sad, lonely life
Of working day and night
For nothing in return

We are bound to a life of slavery

Why?

Alana Francis (13)
The Winston Churchill School

The Ballad Of The Washington Sniper Shootings

There were fourteen attacks
Nine people were killed
They knew their attacker's
Life was fulfilled.

The people of Washington
Hide behind their cars
Hoping that their killer
Will be put behind bars.

The first attack was safest
No one was hurt
A window was smashed
It put them on alert.

The detectives and FBI
Were at a dead-end
They couldn't find the killer
That had put lives to an end.

They called in hypnotists
To jog people's minds
What would have happened
If people's minds were blind?

Activities stopped
All because of two men
Who made a capital
Come to an end, but until when?

There were fourteen attacks
Nine people were killed
They knew their attacker's
Life was fulfilled.

Stephanie Clifford (13)
The Winston Churchill School

Mugs Of Hot Chocolate Are Boring

Mugs of hot chocolate are boring,
Unless they are placed comfortably by a roaring fire,
And the cat comes and curls up on your lap, yawning sweetly.

Trees are pointless.

Unless they are lit by a rising sun,
And the gold of their leaves is highlighted in basking glory.

The sea is plain.

Unless its waves of white horses curl majestically,
Tossing their foaming manes, in a burst of spray

Rides in the country are foolish.

Unless it is a spring afternoon.
And you have a large hamper with a red and white checked
picnic blanket.

A stream is unwanted.

Unless it ripples calmly down a valley,
And cascades over smooth stones, sparkling in the sunshine.

Snow is not festive.

Unless it crunches under your foot,
And glitters in wintry sunshine,
Resting on the leaves of all the trees.

Mountains are worthless.

Unless they dominate the sky for miles,
And are capped with snow,
And their colours run in blues and purples and greys.

Teddies bring no comfort.

Unless they are old and worn,
And a hundred memories are stored in their fur.

Paintings are no joy.

Unless they are true to heart,
With messages hidden a mile within,
For some to see and some to miss.

Rachel Peat (12)
The Winston Churchill School

The Poachers

There were two poachers called John and Pam
Caught stealing for their daily ham
Crime never pays for poachers these days
There was a place where poachers went
Called the forest of ragged tent
Crime never pays for poachers these days
While hunting they chased a deer
In the forest but the owner was near
Crime never pays for poachers these days
They cornered the big hind
Then Pam looked behind
Crime never pays for poachers these days
This thing was chasing her, is what she saw
This thing was a big, fat, ugly boar
Crime never pays for poachers these days
So they galloped off without the deer
And they got home and that was near
Crime never pays for poachers these days
They almost got caught in the pig's pen
But they ran and left the gate open
Crime never pays for poachers these days
What happened was all the pigs escaped
Angry was the farmer Ned
Crime never pays for poachers these days
The police caught John and Pam
They were killed 'chissam'
Crime never pays for poachers these days
There is no moral, there is no reason
Why you should poach any season.

Rebecca Smith (12)
The Winston Churchill School

You

Everywhere I go,
I see your face.
In every corner,
In every place.

Wherever I am,
Here or there.
I know that you
Will always care.

You were great at this
And that and cards.
You always knew
How to have a laugh.

I wish you were
Here with me still,
To make me smile
When I am ill.

Wherever I am,
Whoever I become,
You will always be
My number *one!*

Hollie Tongue (12)
The Winston Churchill School

Cinderella, The True Story

Cinderella was washing the floor
When someone rang the door
Cinderella went to the door and looked on the floor

Cinderella jumped with delight as she saw the letter on the floor
She had always wanted to go to the ball
But alas the ugly stepmum said 'No, go walk the dogs on the moor'
Cinderella sighed and obeyed thinking
Why am I so poor?

Suddenly a fairy popped out of the blue, her name was Sue
Sue granted her wish and made her a coach
And a gown also wearing a crown
Cinderella danced with the prince
And sucked mints until the clock struck 12
She ran for the door dropping her glass slipper on the floor

Oh, the prince was coming, this was a good time to start running
Cinderella ran for the coach but tripped over her cloak
She gulped as the prince saw her in her rags with paper bags
'Burgh, you look like a hag'
And went back to dance with the ugly sisters

So there you have it, the *true* story of Cinderella
And I tell you one thing, the fairy lost her job.

Kaley Groves (12)
The Winston Churchill School

King Henry VIII

King Henry VIII liked to date
King Henry VIII liked to mate
King Henry VIII liked to hunt
King Henry VIII liked watching stunts
King Henry VIII liked being king
King Henry VIII liked to sing
He had a knight who liked to fight
He had a daughter called Mary and she was very scary
He had a daughter who liked to slaughter
He destroyed the church and crumbled it to dirt
He said to the Pope that he was a joke
He had a fat belly and it wobbled like jelly
He had a son who died really young
He had big feasts and ate like a beast

He loved building up big forces
He loved riding magnificent horses
He had six wives: divorced, beheaded, died, divorced,
                                    beheaded, survived,
He took herbal medicine to make it easier to catch venison.

Tom Still (12)
The Winston Churchill School

Sweetie Feast

You're all invited to my house today,
Come in, it's free and you don't have to pay.
The door will be open so in you come
And cram all this chocolate into your tum!

My house will be full of goodies to share,
So come on into my huge choccie lair.
Bring all the sweets that will fit in your truck,
Dive into the sweet tin, it's just pot luck!

Last year a boy came, he ate till he dropped,
Then, like a balloon, he suddenly popped!
I've been hoping no one will burst today,
Cos it took ages to clear the mess away!

Lizzie John (13)
The Winston Churchill School

The Promise

There he stood with an evil, twisted look in his eye,
After stepping down from his noble steed,
Every footstep echoed through the woods,
As a groaning was heard on the edge of the brisk breeze.

Knock, knock upon the old oak door,
No answer, but surely he must be here?
There was no way he would destroy his promise now,
Yet still, knock, knock, no answer.

No noise apart from the phantoms haunting his mind,
The spirits of the house were the only ones to keep him company now,
Not even the spiders would dare set foot in this house,
Oh the horrific tales told about this house years ago.

No noise as he walked down the crooked winding path,
He lifted himself up onto his silent horse
And as he rode off into the distance,
Had the promise finally been broken?

James Trimm (11)
Wallington County Grammar School

Ghoti Ghost

The ghost of the Ghoti sweeps the ground
Silently creeping not making a sound
Tricking its victims and lookers in sure
The sea is its homeland, the ocean floor

When it is midnight the people all shout
'Look out! Look out! The ghost is about'
Planning its time to pounce and strike
All of these people won't live the night

A cry out of the window, a shed tear
These are the signs the Ghoti is here
A laugh or a song is rarely heard
Or a cry of just one bird

The chills on the spine you get when it strikes
Children's blood and flesh - that's what it likes
Its eating cavern under the sea
When you are dying you will so plea

Whether you are alive or you are dead
The next thing you'll see is its big fat head
When you're at town or out at sea
Whatever you do, don't look for me

I am the Ghoti.

Thomas Cole (11)
Wallington County Grammar School

The Tribe Of 10,000,000

They walked together as a crowd,
Standing tall and proud. Ten million, ten million.

They walked through buildings, farms and towns,
One by one they each got lost,
Finding places dark and cold.
Nine million, nine million.

They all came through as part of one.
When suddenly, they all got lost.
Eight million, eight million.

They came together once again,
But this time less and fewer men.
Seven million, seven million.

Finally, they've seen what has happened,
Some have got lost, they were not women.
Six million, six million.

They tumbled down, in a shaped sphere.
It kept on rolling, thousands lost.
Five million, five million.

They came out of the ball, some hurt and bloody.
Found a pub and all went in as one.
Some attacked from behind, others ran.
Four million, four million.

As you know there has been a crime, a murderer is here,
It's not very nice.
They all scattered, finding their way helplessly.
Three million, three million.

They came as one, yet again not knowing who's who.
They approached the leader.
All they yelled was four words:
'Two million, two million.'

They cried and sobbed here and there,
When one huge tribe was put down.
Ten million to one. All that is left is one sad and sorrowful man . . .

The leader!

Osman Oozeerally (11)
Wallington County Grammar School

The Traveller's Return

He turned to tap the door once more,
Tap, tap, tap,
The souls that lay silent inside,
Keeping all noise to a minimum;
The scraggy trees whistled privately,
An old and ongoing song;
'I have done the deed you wanted done my lady'
But no one ever heard;
This baffled soldier knocked once more,
Knock, knock, knock;
Still the rested listened,
Waiting for the death of the silence;
Why did no one come and hear a brave soldier's tale;
How he'd won the battle he'd been given,
Courageously tussling till victory;
Maybe something terrible happened while he trekked,
Into forbidden unknown;
He ran from this place forever,
Not knowing what happened to his mistress.

Adam Kelly (11)
Wallington County Grammar School

Food

Food is oh so lovely,
It's really, really nice,
There's chicken, ham and turkey
And pasta, cheese and rice.

There's sandwiches of bacon,
Marmalade and jam,
Also, courtesy of pigs, is
Delicious pork and ham.

There's fish 'n' chips with ketchup,
Salt and mushy peas too,
Fizzy drinks and cola,
But these are just a few!

For there are fried tomatoes,
Sausages and egg,
Worcester sauce on cheese on toast,
I'm not pulling your leg!

There is spaghetti Bolognese,
With a sauce and mince,
All the food I like to eat,
Make me feel like a prince!

So I would appreciate a dish,
If you're in a giving mood,
'Cause I really, really, really, really,
Really do love food!

Sammy El-Bahrawy (12)
Wallington County Grammar School

Midnight Call

A loud howling pierced the stillness of the night.
Waking many, the call hypnotised the woken.
In the murkiness of foulsome woods,
A white blur silently ran through the crispy leaves of autumn.

Sleepwalking out of their houses to the beckoning woods
Were men of every age,
Dazed in slumber - they had slept their final night.
In power and might the beast was ready to fight.

Deep in the woods, all the men awoke
Remembering too late the warning tale of old.
No weapons to fight with, every man confused,
Swiftly they fell, one by one, stricken by the unseen foe.

And a bell tolled . . .

Joshua Beer (11)
Wallington County Grammar School

I Loved You

When you said we had to part
I tell you it broke my heart
For you were loving, true and kind
Another love like you I will never find
As I walked slowly home
I thought that you might phone
Into the kitchen to get a knife
I had decided to take my life
Three drops of blood fell to the floor
Then you shouted through the door
'Can't we be lovers once more?'
Even with your loving charms
I later died in your arms.

Kareem James-Friday (12)
Wallington County Grammar School

My Football Team

My football team is the best,
Better than all the rest,
I'll support them,
Whatever the weather,
I will be there.

I go there every week to watch them play,
Sometimes they win, sometimes they lose,
The excitement and the buzz,
The cheering supporters,
The build up of the match
With the cheerleaders dancing
And the mascots waving.

The stands are a mass of claret and blue,
The cheers get louder,
Our team emerges,
The whistle blows,
The match starts.
I sit down and stand up,
I cannot keep still,
As half-time arrives, it's nil-nil,
The match starts again and my heart is pounding,
I shout and sing football songs,
The time goes so fast
And it's the end of the match,
I'll be back next week to support them again.

Lawrence Wild (11)
Wallington County Grammar School

Namàrië!

There once was a time, long ago,
when the sun was young,
it shone in the valleys, the hills and the mountains.
It lit the world, preparing it,
for what was soon to come.

There came a people, fair to look upon,
Their hair, silver blonde,
Their eyes, deep blue,
Their figure, tall, sleek and graceful,
Their voices, like sweet music to the ears.
Long they dwelt on this earth, peaceful, joyful, content.

In forests they lived, under their beloved sun, there they sang with
Silky voices and their trees of beauty, elegance and fragrance
Reflected in their silvery thread-like streams into the sun's eyes.

One morning, singing softly to the sun, they heard it cry out,
Its voice full of grief, anger and distress.
'Alas darkness is coming, from the east a black shadow falls on
The blue sky, engulfing all in death and decay, alas!
You must go now my friends, sail away to the undying west,
My time is up, alas, I knew this day would come
But when I could not tell, go . . .'

So as the fair forest-folk
Departed from their ancient homelands
And reached the shores of the far west,
They sang their songs of love and sorrow for their sun.

Roddy Allan (13)
Wallington County Grammar School

A Better Place

The cold air shivers our hero's spine, rivets of ice plunging deep into
flamboyant flesh,
The words of the weak, naïve, destitute of empathy.
Limp-wristed, weak-hearted, down-trodden, our hero must endure the
brick wall of torment, cemented with ignorant prejudice.

Brats smirk as he treads upon cracks, their pavement cracked, their
society cracked,
His life.
Proud he struts from this, vilifying it in his mind, the self-image of self-
important.

Society should be grateful for his perfection.
Never stumbling, never corrupting, never doubting his innate
flawlessness, like a diamond devoid of spectrum. His path should not
be interrupted; no one should behold such audacity.

Halt!
A sight so sorry to have been seen. A white kitten lies dead, lying in his
path. Its blue eyes glazed over, more asleep than deceased.

He holds it in his arms.
Such loss from this world to see these serene creature no more.
No wounds, no blood, no pain, an exit from this world of torture.
He parallels himself with this kitten, both lives marginalised.

In debt to himself, our hero buries the kitten.
The white fur is dirtied when he puts the body below.
He stares jealously at the resting kitten,
Knowing its death was a product of society, a natural end triggered
somehow.

Our hero reveals a knife, the serrated edge of salvation.
Native hatred burns for the kitten, himself and society. He alone knows
what is right.

Putting the knife to his forearm, he opens the vein.
Blood pours, our hero screams, he continues to slit his other wrist.
The bloodied knife impales itself in the ground.
He hunkers next to the kitten's open grave, pleased with his freedom.

Never have two been so polarised.

Kieran Richardson (16)
Wallington County Grammar School

Fear

The emptiness in our minds
The abyss slowing growling
It brings terror and chaos
Can be traumatic to all
The result of wars and slaughter

We all have our phobias
Scaring us to death
Our eyes open wide
We gape at the terror
As it swallows us whole

The omnipresent devil
In a corner of our minds
Eating at the boldness
Damaging our courage

We all fear something
Never leaving us
Taking us to death
The omnipotent fear.

Alexander Max-Lino (12)
Wallington County Grammar School

The Steal

I walked into the stop,
A tingle in my spine.
I looked nervously around,
The shopkeeper thought everything was fine.

My friends looked at me from outside,
I looked at the pack of gum,
It was right at the back of the shop,
My hands were beginning to get numb.

I asked, 'How much is the gum?'
He said, '30p!'
I picked it up and then thought,
Is this the real me?

I grabbed the packet and read the label,
The time was getting near,
I walked towards the door, my friends smiled,
Suddenly I gave it to the cashier!

I reached out for my pocket,
Handed him thirty pence,
Then I thought,
Where was the sense?

I walked out of the shop
Without a care in the world
And with a lot of relief!
I was not, am not
And definitely will not be a *thief!*

Pirasannah Jeyadeva (11)
Wallington County Grammar School

Exams

An exaggerated sound of footsteps,
Echoing around the hall.
Everyone's eardrums began to wobble,
As they wait to hear the call.

They sprint down the corridor to the hall,
To get their test results.
They strained their ears to hear the teacher's voice,
They waited in silence.

They listened hard for their own test results,
The standard was not high.
Must try harder to be the best in class,
To earn our teacher's praise.

Studying became very popular,
To increase our results.
Teachers wanted us to be successful
And to achieve our goal.

It's June, the end of year tests has arrived,
This time we have revised.
We hope we have done enough to succeed
And will receive our prize.

David Young (12)
Wallington County Grammar School

Plants Swaying In The Wind

As I gazed through my bedroom window
Staring into oblivion
I watched birds fly, cats play and dogs bark
As I waited until it got dark

I wished I wasn't grounded for saying something rude
I did apologise
But that wasn't quite sufficient
Next time I'll try and word it different

The plants swayed backwards and forwards
The leaves went up and down
They looked like people dancing
Or even soldiers marching

Although it was dark, it left its mark and still the wind blew
I noticed the plants swaying in the wind
It looked so peaceful, as I was gazing
. . . I found it quite amazing.

Jordan Macauley (11)
Wallington County Grammar School

The Grey Mist

The grey mist bloomed over the city,
It was like a patch of darkness had taken over,
We were all trapped in the gloominess.
People were getting very aggressive,
Many fights had occurred.
I knew there was still some hope,
I stood there thinking, why?
Just when everything seemed down,
I saw a glimmer or a shine,
But when I approached,
It was only someone's tear.

Arpit Patel (12)
Wallington County Grammar School

Snow

Snow tastes like
Nippy frozen salt;
Our snow tastes like
What is a revolting sour mint.

Snow feels like
Numbing icy golf balls;
Our snow feels like
Walnut-like meatballs although much softer.

Snow looks like a
Neat lump of cotton wool;
Our snow looks like
Woolly, fluffy clouds only more spheres.

Snow sounds like
Navy-blue empty bags being stamped on;
Our snow sounds like
Walking people strolling through mud.

Snow smells like
New fresh country air;
Our snow smells like
Wintry pieces of frosted grass.

Julien Appadurai (11)
Wallington County Grammar School

Sailing

The wind in the sails, the water in the lake,
Silence all around apart from this,
This boat, my boat,
Sailing with friends in the one lake,
In the district of lakes,
The smooth cool water
And then,
Man overboard, man overboard,
The wind suddenly fell,
That poor sailor swim could he not,
Under he plunged,
Then it struck me, in I went,
Under I went,
I had him in my arms,
When I rose he was breathing,
The boat, where was it?
The wind must have struck when I was under,
Someone in a motorboat was zooming up the lake,
It was Dad,
'Ahoy, ahoy.'
And over he came,
Up we climbed soaking but saved.

Stephen Mann (12)
Wallington County Grammar School

Winter

Freezing blue-white of winter chill,
Soft, icy cold snow,
Hail clattering at the window,
All belong to winter.

Puddles turning to ice,
Silence on the frozen roads,
Fires roaring in every fireplace,
All belong to winter.

Snowmen tall and cold,
Snowballs flying through the air,
Frosty breath in the cold outside,
All belong to winter.

Love and joy on Christmas Day,
Celebrations at New Year,
Hats and coats and gloves and scarves,
All belong to winter.

Alexander Clarke (12)
Wallington County Grammar School

My Midnight Mind

My midnight mind
Strong, relaxing, proud
Brings possible from impossible
Mixes dreams with reality.
I live in new life at night,
Every day live something new,
Enchanted, cool, calm,
Mountains ice-white,
To sand dunes yellow,
My midnight mind,
Always, never-ending.

Mohammed Faisal Suleman (12)
Wallington County Grammar School

War On A Small Screen

I saw the box,
It looked interesting,
It looked fun,
I turned it on,
Had a go,
But was soon to realise,
That it showed war as it wanted to be seen,
Proud,
Happy,
Simple,
But there was none of the pain,
The suffering,
The brave soldiers marching forth,
Faces grim with determination,
Over land,
Sea
And air,
In grinning machines of death,
Or on foot
Only to meet their doom
Or to cause the doom of others.

Andrew Hatcher (13)
Wallington County Grammar School

Age

How age comes we will never know,
It comes with our slightest breath,
Until at last we finally go,
Embraced by eternal death.

When people die, relatives grieve,
They are lost and beginning to mourn,
For this there can be no reprieve,
So they'll cry for their loved ones
Beneath the lawns.

Jack Baker (12)
Wallington County Grammar School

Silence

The world has accepted,
That there is no such thing as silence,
Something that is slowly forced out of our lives.

Like an unwanted child,
An abandoned house,
A neglected forest,

Silence is peace.
Peace is silence.
We don't know silence,
How can we bring peace
And stop all the violence and chaos?

We won't.
We don't.

We crave silence and peace.
We cannot have it.
We do not want anger and war,
Though we have it.

We want what we cannot have.
We have what we do not want.

Silence is calm,
Silence is painful,

Silence does not exist.

Uche Ogbuagu (12)
Wallington County Grammar School

What Is Silence?

Noiseless noise,
Soundless sound.
Emptiness in which sound has been devoured.
A pinnacle of quiet, which noise can never reach.
A state that cannot exist,
Or be proved.

More fragile than glass,
Faster than sound.
A murmur, then silence is broken.
Sound catches up, now silence has lost.

More free than the wind,
Silence cannot be witnessed.
Trying to witness silence,
Chases it further away.
Only trekking away from life,
Where noise is eternal,
Is where you will finally meet silence.

Gianluca Ivaldi (13)
Wallington County Grammar School

Streets

Among the busy streets
In the middle of town
Is a flowery field
Where houses have been knocked down

Men with cranes and bulldozers
Left the grounds brown and bare
Except for the broken bricks
Scattered everywhere

The ground was rough and bumpy
And there the old bricks lay
Like a construction set
That hadn't been put away.

Stuart Young (12)
Wallington County Grammar School

Winter Poem

Grey, blue, white,
Cold, dark, wet,
Trees bare,
The land is still,

Winter has come,
It has scattered the lands with icing,
A carpet of coloured leaves lies beneath the trees,
Sharp pointed icicles hang from gutters waiting to drop,

There is a chill in the air,
The cold breath of winter whispering in my ear,
Its hands clench me icy and cold,
Its claws chill and bite in the bitter air,

It beats with its hands against me,
It whips up my coat with its cold breath,
It howls at me in the night through the gaps in the windows,
But its chilling breath and beating fists will not reach me anymore.

Max Nuttall (12)
Wallington County Grammar School

The Snake

A giant snake lived in a cave in Spain,
He gave the scared village a lot of pain,
He hissed when he was hungry and caused trouble,
As the snake slithered through the rubble,
He filled the villagers with dread,
The little children fled,
He munched on a juicy rat,
As the snake felt rather fat,
As sly as a fox, he began to feel sleepy,
Overjoyed that the giant snake had left them,
As they found him extremely creepy,
Clapping and laughter was heard in the village.

Richard Bridger (11)
Wallington County Grammar School

The Water's Poem

I have been around the world many times,
As many different forms,
Ice, water and vapour
Are all forms of me!

As ice I glisten an icy blue,
I'm cold to the touch
And fresh to the taste,
Water and vapour are other forms of me!

As water I fill the sea,
I'm 70 percent of the Earth,
So people must see me!
Ice and vapour are other forms of me!

As vapour I fill the air all around,
I can't be seen and I don't make a sound!
I create clouds in the sky up high,
Ice and water are other forms of me!

I have been around the world many times,
As many different forms,
Ice, water and vapour
Are all different forms of me!

Thomas Wood (12)
Wallington County Grammar School

Sleep

Complete and utter nothingness,
Befalls you,
When your head
Touches your pillow.

Like a blanket
Of darkness,
Covers you from
Head to toe.

But on this dark blanket
Are stories and dreams,
Stories of wonder,
Fantasy, fiction and truth.

Fire-breathing dragons,
Knights in shining armour,
Princesses locked in the tallest tower
Or brave men fighting evil.

But soon enough,
This dark blanket
Is lifted and
Light creeps in the room.

Dominic Bell (12)
Wallington County Grammar School

Arctic

This is where polar bears walk,
Cold, bitter, icy blue,
Everything white as chalk,
Oh I wish I was back with you.

Everything is ice,
Birds fly away from here,
It is far from nice,
Too scared to shed a tear.

Animals staring,
All with their beady eyes,
For their prey they are preparing,
Waiting for a surprise.

Polar bears roaring
With their frightening tone,
They're always watching, never boring,
All *alone!*

Daniel Siggs (12)
Wallington County Grammar School

The Egg

An egg is like the world,
We have the power to destroy it,
We can make its future,
This power is used in the real world.

Eggs will break - if forced to;
Like the world - if it is pushed too far.
In the real world things change,
Just like an egg if it has been cooked.
An egg is like the world,
The power of it is in our hands.

Tayo Ologbenla (12)
Wallington County Grammar School

The Snow

Soft, delicate, plain drifted from the sky.
Trampled on carelessly like an uncared-for flower in a dark, damp
place.
Slowly, piece by piece, this work of art falls down,
Hitting the ground like it's a victim plunged to their death.

Waves around like a dancer performing her dance,
Twirling, whirling and whizzing round and round.
A little girl acting innocent and sweet,
Little droplets of pureness falling from the sky.

Day by day, hour by hour, this beauty is restored,
Filling our hearts with joy and love,
This beautiful object that can bring happiness to this world.

Falling like a soft air-bound stampede,
Rushing like there is a race to be won.
Glistening trees as if a family holiday is coming,
The day of joy has come.

The snow flying through the air,
Following the wind like a sheep,
The wind is filled with cold,
The wind is filled with joy.

Day by day, hour by hour, this beauty is restored,
Filling our hearts with joy and love,
This beautiful object that can bring happiness to this world,
This one thing is snow.

Hans Laud-Anderson (12)
Wallington County Grammar School

Differences

Wet, cold, bluish ice,
Dry, hot, reddish spice,
Gushing, flushing, H_2O,
Blowing, flowing, helps to grow.

Melodious, mellow, jam tart,
Bitter, acid, vinegary, sharp,
Saline, briny, salty, crunching,
Chomping, chewy, gooey, munching.

Fragile, brittle, titch, small,
Sly, clever, slick, cool,
Vicious, strong, angry, wild,
Huge, fat, tough, mild.

Grass, leaves, peas, broccoli,
Water, sky, lapis lazuli,
Sun, lemon, sand, chips,
Rubies, peppers, blood, lips.

White, black, brown, mixed,
Christian, Hindu, Muslim, Jew,
Blonde, ginger, curly, fixed,
Is there any difference?

Matthew Clare (12)
Wallington County Grammar School

Leap

We all have hopes, we all have dreams
But are these things floating in our minds
Crazy and demented wishes as they seem
No! If we leap out that's what we'll find

You may believe you cannot win
Or do the thing you'd like to do
My answer to this is to find within
Your thoughts and fantasies meant for you

Build them up and hold them inside
Take these with you and make a leap
Think of the way we would glide
And then land safely upon your feet

For of course there is no harm in trying
At what you've always wished to do
You will feel like you are flying

On your thoughts and fantasies . . . meant for only you.

Thomas Evans (13)
Wallington County Grammar School

Snow

Snow drifts down from the sky,
Something catches my eye,
Snow trickles down from the rooftops,
Onto the icy floor,
A football lays perished in white, soft snow,
Children laugh and giggle,
As they throw snowballs at each other,
While parents sit by a cosy fire,
With a cup of tea clenched in their hands,
While I stare through the misty windowpane
And wish I were inside again.

Ben McDaniel (11)
Wallington County Grammar School

Snowflakes

Snowflakes are white and cold,
They are also so light
And very quick to melt.
They are extremely small,
Also microscopic.

Snowflakes are very chilled,
Like realistic gold.
There is a good amount
That always keeps falling.

It is dull when snowflakes
Keep thudding on your neck.
It is always freezing cold
When it keeps hitting you
In the same old place.

Lakshman Vigneswaran (11)
Wallington County Grammar School

The Black Hole

The black hole,
So dark and mysterious,
Never-ending and eternal.
Where does it lead to?
Nobody knows.
Objects and planets
Get pulled into it,
Where do they go?
Nobody knows.
Some so small,
Smaller than a dot,
But still,
They drag whole planets and stars
Into the doom,
That is their wrath.

Tom Hammond (11)
Wallington County Grammar School

A Virgin With Child

The lady with the golden hair
Cradles her baby in her arms,
She's rocking the child so it sleeps,
She is in need of harmony and peace.

In the distance there appears a forest,
With the rustling sounds echoing around her,
Her hair is blowing to the tunes
Of the sounds around her.

A tear begins to slowly fall,
I wonder why she cries?
Is this tear a tear of joy
Or is there sadness in her heart?

The baby is now fast asleep
As the mother sits and stares,
The tears begin to fade away
And the light behind begins to dim.

Marc Goodwin (13)
Wallington County Grammar School

Uniform

A man stands clutching his rifle, his eyes full of fear.
All around utter chaos, mud, the smell of blood.
Shells streak across the sky like comets,
Explosions light up the faces of soldiers like a firework display.

Across no-man's-land, two miles away, another man stands,
Clutching his rifle. His eyes are full of fear.
He misses his family, a distant memory.
Which man is British? Which man is German?
Which man is good? Which man is evil?
The only difference between them is their uniform.

Joshua Roberts (12)
Wallington County Grammar School

Evil Grannies

If ya gran's not being too nice
An' nickin' all ya games dat you bought at a high price
An' if she's showing all ya mates ya baby pictures
An' telling dat your dad left ya mum to become a hitcher

Well don't take none of dat, it ain't right,
You gotta kick her inda hip an' put up a fight.
If she spills some juice on ya new mat,
All ya gotta do is run over her cat.

If ya nan comes over with some boof,
'N' goes, 'I'm gunna kick ya inda front tooth,'
Kick her right back in da head,
But make sure you don't hit her so hard dat she'll be dead.

As well if she sees ya 'n' goes 'Wanna piece of me?'
Go, 'Yeah, wotever Nana, just not your dodgy left knee.'
You should only do this is ya nan's possessed,
Or got *die grandson, die* tattooed across her chest.

Nathan Atkinson (14)
Wallington County Grammar School

Sun Bad, Sun Good

It is a great big yellow ball
If we get too close, it will roast us all

It just sits there; the world does all the turning
It lights our life, every morning

The sun on your back puts a smile on your face
It's the light of our lives, from outer space

It turns some people golden brown and brings out freckles in others
Dark skins can soak up the sun, but pale skins must take cover

Icarus thought he was a bit of a lad
He flew too close and it got bad

Melted wings, unable to fly
If you mess with the sun then you will *die!*

Alexander Pridding (11)
Wallington County Grammar School

Running Man

The road stretched out to the end of sight,
The colours blurred in the midday heat,
The road was red, the floor, yellow,
But still the man let for no respite.

He was running; from people, from life,
He could not get away - they refused to leave.
Nothing would change,
So he ran - from nothing, from everything.

He would not allow himself to stop,
For the road still stretched out,
The memories still too fresh,
The haunting still too near.

And so he ran!
Giving himself no respite,
Pushing himself further,
For the road still lay out ahead.

James Barnett (13)
Wallington County Grammar School

The Traveller's Return

Only last night the traveller returned,
As his horse thundered down the dusty track
Towards the vacant house.
He dismounted and pounded on the unused door,
Thumping again and again.
The traveller would not leave though,
Promises aren't for the breaking.
Had there been a misunderstanding?
For there was no sign of life here.
Then he heard an unsettling sound,
The sheer emptiness of the place was enough to scare you away.
He leapt onto his horse and thundered along the dusty track,
The door opened slowly
And a head peered into the moonlight.

Andrew Lill (11)
Wallington County Grammar School

From The Cradle To Enslave

Isolation is such a lonely place,
Death, hunger, eternal darkness,
You'll know the level of pain by the sound of this scream,
I put my left foot forward and fall.

A baron's barren castle lies alone,
He loves none, feels none, is none,
A pile of corpses, I'm at the bottom of the top,
Beelzebub fled from this place so should I.

Blasphemous pig, a scoundrel, a man of hate,
Killed my people, but me, I was special, this is my fate,
Darkness feels my soul, he beckons me,
He wants my blood. He is immortal, a grave digger.

Me, him and Lucifer, the dark trinity
Of martyrs and men with their sinful nature,
Like a wolf among the flock, rival the eminent,
I bring them down to a new height. I am hate.

Sam McKavanagh (13)
Wallington County Grammar School

Anthem Of A Doomed Yute

(Inspired by 'Anthem For Doomed Youth')

What hope is there for those who live in shadows,
Where brothers and sisters fall like tears?
In the streets, where sound is non-existent save footsteps
And change and loose chains are objects of desire.
Suffering post death received as 'emotional'
And where peers may just as well be foes.
In the old recreation ground,
Where gangs of men relax with rolled herbs,
To relieve deep pressures, deep stresses,
When deep breathing is no longer the solution
And the youth strolls by, unshaken by their gazes,
But wanders to his place in the far corner,
With red eyes chasing him past.

Tetevi Davi (13)
Wallington County Grammar School

What I Created

What went wrong?
I thought I left it perfect,
How could things come so undone?
Where has all the love gone?

The rich are getting richer,
The poor even poorer;
Instead of fighting a war on poverty,
They got a war on the Pakistanis,

So the hate revolves back to me,
In my time, when I tried for peace,
But the country was still on a lease,
What was a man to do?

Thought I conquered corruption,
Thought I defeated greed,
Learned to live as a single nation,
But I guess, that was then, they were led by me.

Vinith Pillai (13)
Wallington County Grammar School

The Evil Today

In the night while all is dead
It covers the world like a flood
As morning comes all is gone
All but this feeling of dread

As it takes a stranglehold
What do we try and do?
Do we try and put up a fight
Or do we back down out of fright?

This is the choice you have to make
Don't make your choice out of haste
This choice could seal your fate
Or help you to taste

That sweet thing called *victory.*

Joshua Bridgeman (13)
Wallington County Grammar School

Snowflakes

Sugary, sweet, soft and cold
snowflakes are lighter than feathers,
gentler than a mother's touch.

Floating on the wind's breath,
they pass by our faces,
as they swoop down to the cold ground,
patiently painting the Earth's floor white.

At the start of winter a single snowflake falls
and then another and another,
until the sky is coloured in white,
while silver clouds float lazily by.

The signs of Christmas are finally here,
the snowflakes seem like messengers,
drifting through the country,
bringing joy to all that behold her,
as she tells of the joy and hope that Christmas brings.

Soon the winter breeze subsides
and the flakes disappear,
one by one,
melting, sliding, slipping to the other world,
until the cold air of winter
is the only thing that's left.

Jamal Beckford (11)
Wallington County Grammar School

The Midnight Flight

They had to go, they had no choice,
Before the summer went and the days got moist,
Before the flowers withered and died
And the squirrels went away to hide.

Up they went in a magical formation,
Which in a contest would win the hearts of the nation.
Flying high over many landmarks,
Ducking down low to see the royal parks!
Up, up high over Trafalgar Square,
Whatever people thought, they didn't care!
But none of them forgot where they had to go,
Otherwise they may be caught in the winter's snow.

They felt even more need to carry on,
As the long hours of sunlight would soon be gone,
Some of the group decided to give up,
But many kept going hoping for good luck!
With utmost determination in their eyes,
They pressed on through the dangerous skies.

Then suddenly there it was, the storm,
It lit up the night sky as if it was dawn!
Thunder boomed, rain poured down,
The storm clouds covered them like a gown!

But at the end of the storm only the smallest one remained,
'The king of the skies', he could have claimed!
So on and on he went alone,
Until he saw in the distance his home!
Then eventually he trained all of his children so as they might
One day take *The Midnight Flight!*

Joseph Ros (12)
Wallington County Grammar School

The Silence Is Broken?

What is happening in the world today?
The answer is, people killing people nowadays,
I've been asked by little children
Why people are crying,
And I said because people are dying.

The silence is broken.

Why can't anyone be together?
Why can't children even act, walk and talk together?
Is it just me or is the world falling apart?
Maybe it is,
No, the world can't be falling apart!

The silence is broken.

So much evil filling the hearts of little ones,
Why can't we be nice as the youth are young,
Like the war,
Inflicting children faster than bacteria,
Kids acting like what they see in the cinema,

The silence is broken?

Jordan Braithwaite (11)
Wallington County Grammar School

Silently

Silently people wait for the train,
Silently the wind ruffles a horse's mane,
Silently a man gets a drink,
Silently the children think.

Silently people get better,
Silently a man writes a letter,
Silently the green grass grows,
Silently pimples appear on someone's nose.

William Eggleton (13)
Wallington County Grammar School

The Sensation

I pull out my pale tongue
And suspend it
In the November air.
Stretching my tongue forward
To catch life by the tail.
A snowflake falls slowly,
Hypnotised by the wind,
Shivers twist down my spine -
The snowflake has landed!
The salt and sourness,
The gentle touch fuelling
My burning ecstasy -
It is a great moment.
The taste of pollution
Creeps in the back door,
Discontent arising.
The snowflake has dissolved,
Causing a moment's gap
In my raging heartbeat.
There, on my tongue remains
Salty, murky water -
The sensation ends.

Joseph Ayoola (11)
Wallington County Grammar School

Blizzard

Fast, brief, cold,
Snowflakes hit with ferocious accuracy,
Striking continually without mercy,
Find targets and home in,
Attacking with great skill.

The blizzard rages on,
Vision is blurred,
The cold stings your eyes,
You shut them and wait,
Till the anger of the blizzard passes.

Hailstones join the fray,
Rain, sleet, snow and hailstones attack,
Hurling all they have at the tired,
The weary,
The weak.

The forces surround targets,
Hitting anywhere possible,
The targets walk briskly on,
Head down, taking the blows,
Relentless numbers flow in always attacking.

Suddenly it fades away,
The sky clears, leaving no trace of war.

The forces have gone, but they will be back, always be back.

Nathan Goodman (12)
Wallington County Grammar School

Winter

Plain creamy delight of snow,
The golden pine trees start to glow.
Bright shining colours all around,
My feet can barely touch the ground.

The summer leaves started falling,
Old Jack Frost has begun calling.
The robin redbreast sings with glee,
As if it were talking to me.

The spirit of Christmas is near,
We all begin to have no fear,
Because our friend Santa is here
And stays with us until New Year.

As we look back at Christmas past,
Our minds knew that it would not last.
But winter stays for quite a while
And it always fades with a smile.

Vincenzo Franco (11)
Wallington County Grammar School

Hong Kong

The moist gentle breeze of fresh air,
brushing timidly against my face.
Signs of shops, flashing madly above me,
gritty pavements, packed with people.
Shoes clattering melodically against my ear,
shy market stalls tucked away in dark corners.
Restaurants that swiftly feed people,
like feeding a ferocious pack of lions.
Cars that rush here and there.
This is paradise.
This is Hong Kong.

Anthony Liu (12)
Wallington County Grammar School

The Midnight Call

Little Jonny sat bolt upright,
A very loud noise had given him a fright,
The sound came in the middle of the night.

Little Jonny was stricken with fear,
The yell had seemed to be very near,
Out of his eye slid a little tear.

He listened on to the silence around,
His little heart began to pound,
As he anticipated the next fearful sound.

He decided to out of his room creep,
The next terrifying noise was very deep,
He fell to the floor in a crumpled heap.

Little Jonny's dad came up to see,
Little Jonny was about to flee,
'We were only watching footie on TV.'

Tim Gibson (11)
Wallington County Grammar School

Cold

He floats through the air,
Searching for his next victim.
He sits on haunches,
Waiting to pounce.
The town goes quiet,
Who will he pick? They're waiting.
They sense he is there,
Coiled, ready.
Huddled together,
They feel protected like that.
He chooses his target,
They can only wait.
He slowly stretches.
Now he is toying with them
And then he pounces;
Ghost or spectre?
The cold!

Douglas Still (11)
Wallington County Grammar School

Enemy

My image reflects in the enemy's eyes
and his image reflects in mine the same lies.

Only one of us can live forever,
So you and I can't ride together.
Can't live or can't die together,
All we can do is fight each other.

I against I,
Flesh of my flesh,
Mind of my mind,
Two of a kind but one won't survive.

A doorstep where death always comes,
But I'm never close,
Walk tall, why not ever run?
Will they move if I ever come?

My image reflects in the enemy's eyes
And his image reflects in the enemy's eye.

Rishi Dhokia (13)
Wallington County Grammar School

Teachers!

On Earth they are human beings called teachers
They live in school all year long
You can hear them here, they usually say
'Where has all your homework gone?'

Teachers are funny old people
They come in all shapes and they mime
The things that they teach me really well
Helped me write this terrible rhyme!

Teachers are really quite mad
But that's what this poem's about
The top three things on their 'to do' list
Are shout and shout and shout

One last word about teachers
They sometimes are rather cool
When you get used to their mindless babbling
They give you merits for keeping the rules!

Royzan Ahamadeen (11)
Wallington County Grammar School

The Midnight Call

There I stood listening, listening,
In the midnight breeze.
The mountain top's my home,
My guardian the wind,
Whispering a lullaby between the tops.

There I stood looking, looking,
The moonlight shining,
The rays glistening,
Revealing a spiritual mist,
Shadows engulfing it with darkness.

There I stood changing, changing,
My spirit in the arms of Morpheus,
I began to feel arcane,
I felt an intense urge of hunger,
The midnight call had begun.

Andrew Walsh (11)
Wallington County Grammar School

Teachers: Madame Anonymous

She sits at her desk waiting,
The bell sounds loud and clear,
'Some kids,' she said, 'are late in,
The drongos are not yet here.'

The late ones finally arrive,
She gives them an earful,
They sit and look so deprived,
None of them look too cheerful.

The lesson starts with a couple of lectures,
It almost drives us round the bend,
Our accents have to clearly match hers,
Our translation books, our only friends.

The bell sound a dull, loud drone,
We are surprised we are not dead,
You hear a cheer and then a groan,
We forgot there was a second period ahead.

Matthew Wait (12)
Wallington County Grammar School

All Things Dull And Ugly

Idyllic countryside all around
The grass and trees adorn the ground,
When round the corner, large and green,
A digger with intentions mean.

It starts to excavate the scene,
Smashing trees to make it clean,
It's followed by a building army,
That must be absolutely barmy.

The workers enter thick and fast,
The time of countryside is past.
And there! A brand new factory,
Developers shout and dance with glee.

And with it come the rows of flats,
With dirty alleys, yowling cats.
So much for former countryside,
We humans brushed it all aside.

Dominic Newman (11)
Wallington County Grammar School

Darkness

Darkness, loneliness, as in isolation
And even with friends you can feel all alone,
Guilty feelings can make everything darker
And you can feel as if everything hates you,
Sadness is dark times, nothing's going your way
And it makes it seem to just not blow away.

If you try never to do anything wrong,
Then you will have nothing to worry about,
It's impossible to never commit wrongs,
That means everybody has some guilt in them,
Loneliness is a nasty part of our life,
That is because you have no one to talk with.

Some little people are afraid of the dark,
Because they do not know what is around them,
People get frightened with imaginations,
From scary films and pictures from story books.
Some get frightened when seeing creepy-crawlies,
That's because we don't know a lot about them.

James Hamilton (11)
Wallington County Grammar School

Where Am I?

I come awake in unfamiliar territory,
I am out of place.
Creeping fear and anxiety take over me,
I panic - where am I?
Cold and wet - body trembling,
Hands in front in the dark,
I stumble blindly.
Soft threads brush my face,
A gush of dread crashes in my stomach,
Like tidal waves on shingle.

I feel wood against my palm,
Cautiously I push, a door creaks open.
Underfoot the crunch of leaves
And then moonlight reflected in a window,
Like a beacon guiding me home.
I am in my garden,
My father walks towards me, smiling,
Fear leaves me,
Perhaps for his next victim.

Daniel Bleach (11)
Wallington County Grammar School

Trapped

They'll find me soon, I can feel it,
They'll come in and take me away.
They'll take me to their leader
And I'll be killed the very next day.

I'm all alone in my attic,
Just waiting for them to appear,
Wherever I turn, it's useless,
I'll die there or die here in fear.

The darkness is unbearable
And the silence: I cannot take.
If I just make one single noise,
Then my whole life will be at stake.

I can almost hear them searching:
They're throwing my chairs on the floor,
One's walking up to the attic
And, God! He's opening the door . . .

He'll find me soon, I can feel it,
I'll die and be buried at sea.
But ending a life isn't bad,
When the life wasn't ever free.

Sumil Thakrar (11)
Wallington County Grammar School

Weather

Delicate snow falling gently
On your tongue a slight shiver,
Cold white freezing colour,
Soft and light.

The wind that's older
Than the universe,
Stronger than the land,
Strikes violently at you,
As a hurricane or tornado
And howls like a wolf.

Pinging pin sounds of rain,
Pitter-patter pitter,
Reminds me of sad times,
When I bumped my head.

But the sun is hotter than desert,
That reminds me of good times
And lazing around in the sun
And ice cream.

The crash of lighting is the best,
It is power and chaos,
It reminds me of Zeus and Zulu,
That's why I love the strike of lightning!

Neil Kandiah (11)
Wallington County Grammar School

The Absence Of Light

Beyond all light,
Darkness is there,
Like a bite,
It tears us,
In darkness,
No best exists,
Also,

Where pain lies,
Winter lies,
It brings a
Grim grey of
Corrupted
Light.

Why does God's
Dark brother
Do this to
Us humans?
Eating our
Perfect hearts,
Not giving
It up.

Does God save
Us?
Yes, He does,
He gives us
Hope
To our soul.

Ho-ming Kwong (11)
Wallington County Grammar School

The Promise

The night had arrived completely now, silent as could be,
Apart from the faint sound of hooves in the distance,
They got louder, as it came towards the lonely, forgotten house,
Off went the man, before the horse chomped the moon bathed, green grass,
He turned to the house, his face full of dread and despair,
'I return to you, bad news I bear,' called the man to the house,
No reply came; there was silence once more,
Apart from the horse finishing his midnight meal.
'I have done wrong, I betrayed you without knowing,' he cried once more.
Nothing happened to please the man, he was let down,
'It controlled me, I swear, like the Devil I sinned,' came his bloodthirsty call.
'It is not entirely gone; it still possesses me somewhere,
Although most of it escaped, a little was left behind,
It captured part of my soul, never shall I be free.'
Through a small gap in the tree's bundled leaves,
Moonlight poured through, resting on the man's face,
He turned to the moon, like he knew something strange.
'Tell them it is out, it roams free, never to be caught again,
Tell them I owe so very much, my life I would kindly give.'
He spoke to the moon like it was a friend of his,
He called his horse and it strode over towards him,
He got on and the sounds of hooves were back, as he rode gently away.

Callum McKeown (11)
Wallington County Grammar School

The Unknown

It's coming up the stairs with its slimy feet,
It's coming to get me,
Why is it in the house and not in the street?
I wonder if it's a he or she?

I wonder if I will survive this?
I didn't say anything to anybody today,
Is it his?
Is this my last day?

It has arrived up the stairs,
Is this the end of my life?
I wonder if it has hairs?
I don't want to die before having a wife.

It is starting to open the door,
I went under my bed,
Did it come to my room because I am not poor?
Before I die I would really like a piece of bread.

It started coming in,
I made myself flat,
It was standing next to the bin,
It looked quite fat.

It opened the door completely now,
This was the end,
It kept on making a noise of a cow,
I had to bend.

It saw me,
It came up to me and picked me up,
It opened its mouth,
It put me in its mouth and just swallowed me, where I died.

Mithilan Sivasubramaniyam (11)
Wallington County Grammar School

That Boy Filled With Joy

Silence, calm, soundless, dumb, the fearful and tearful
Had almost begun;
We had been waiting on hand, foot and toe,
For nothing was said,
Until it almost begun.
They kicked forth their kick-starts
And the enthusiasm begun,
To start and then stop,
To wait on the clock,
To feel the heart beating,
Of that boy filled with joy
And to see his pleasurable smile,
Was happy for just new.
The territory of men, to the pit of man's doom
And just as it started,
The expanse filled with fumes,
They were off after waiting,
They were taken down by few,
But the happiness of Michael,
Seemed to caper with no coup,
As everyone turned to see the formidable track,
The motocross nightmare,
Came unlucky for two.
It started off easy and ended up hard,
The impulsive snap of a back;
Was Michael's brother, Carl.
With only one left,
Of one determined, non-aggressive family,
The tears falling down
Of that boy filled with joy.

Jamie Crawford (12)
Wallington County Grammar School

The Killer

The striped fire beast creeps slowly
It crouches as still as a rock
Its target locked
A poor innocent creature
A deer

It happens all too quickly
In a blur of orange and brown
Savage blades thrashing
A sight sickening to watch
I cry out

The piercing yellow eyes flash to me
Its large bloody snout breathing on my face
Fear creeping round me
Its mouth opens
Darkness

The killer walks off into the jungle
As my head rolls into the distance
The same fate shall fall on another person
To the wrath of the
Tiger!

Nicholas Tomlin (12)
Wallington County Grammar School

Life

First the baby small and precious,
With tiny hands and tiny feet,
Crying and wailing except when asleep.

Then the child youthful and light-hearted,
With glistening blue eyes and a handsome face.

The teenager grumpy and moody,
Yet kind and searching for love.

The third age passes and reveals marriage,
Joy fills the air,
The wedding bells ring,
But soon joy will turn to sorrow.

A split appears as death takes its toll,
Two becomes one.

Now alone and feeble,
The decrepit old man awaits his future.
Light dims, sound fades,
Memory lives strong but touch is no more.

Darkness looms and death prevails.

Thomas Bedford (13)
Wallington County Grammar School

The Promise

Trees swishing back and forth,
Leaves crackling amongst the breeze,
Where was the destination?
Wolves howling under the sunlit sky,
Dim, but burning the weather went on.

I told her in trust that I would return,
The journey's made me dazed and confused.
Where was the destination?
Barriers blocking the forward paths,
But I fight myself to keep going.

I once lived here happy and peaceful,
Why did I ever leave
Where was the destination?
What stupid mistakes ran through my head,
I regret the howler that changed it all.

Suddenly a ray of sun shone through the dark clouds,
A presence of hope came to join me,
Was this the destination?
Darkness appeared, I fell to the floor,
The promise was too late . . .

Jordan Tuboly (11)
Wallington County Grammar School

The TV

It was Tuesday, one minute to six and Neighbours was over long ago
When the TV made a funny noise, or was it just the next show?
But for all that I would know,
Next to me were Tinky Winky, Dipsy, Laa-Laa and Po!
They took me over the lush green hill and into a dome-shaped home,
I was taken to their slide, up they went one by one,
I sat down and *whoh!*

And there was Bella, what has happened here?
Their clock was flashing and then it stopped
And they were marching on the spot,
My feet started moving, no, not here.

The floor started to crumble and there were the big 'fun' Fimbles!
There were three of them with a bird, a mole and a frog.
They took me to their tinkling tree and how 'untinkily' it was.
Then to their delight a dying, wilted plant they found
Sprawled out on the ground,
Then they found the 'water' and watered the wrinkly thing.
Then they all ran over to the old mole on a swing,
The mole read them a story, *zzzzzzzz*, where am I?
Oh, I dreamt the whole stupid thing!

So next time, don't fall asleep in your chair,
Or you may end up in Toyland with Noddy and Tubby Bear!

Stuart Clarke (11)
Wallington County Grammar School

Apocalypse

The time for destruction has come
So you'd better start to run
The curse has come upon the world
It's ending faster than it swirled
The seven skies have gone grey with envy
The sun has turned from one too many
The cellars of evil titans are opened
The wonderful promises of angels are broken
Mummies, zombies and the dead have woken
The god has now stepped and spoken
The universe has now come to an end
The death at every corner but no friend
The moon has turned from golden to red
The meteors are showering while you are in bed
The stars are exploding, the planets are dropping
The millions and billions of asteroids are bombing
But there is always a reward for people who have hope
Which is to go to Heaven and be a pope
So up you go, the chosen ones
Into the sky of the mighty one.

Fatik Bashir (12)
Wallington County Grammar School

The Midnight Call

He rode up to the formation of stones,
The night gloomy and dull,
For no longer was the horse normal,
For the horse he had departed on,
Its skin made of dark and shady tones,
Had turned into flesh and worn-down weak bones.

The house ahead had been neglected,
In a battle it was affected,
It was a shame that the house which was awkward,
In the past years had been bewildered,
The secure door shaded in brown,
But it made reverberated as if it was going to fall down.

He perched on a smooth flat stone,
Then he relaxed and made himself feel at home,
For a man came hobbling in,
His face old and dim,
'Where is it?' the wrinkled old man proclaimed,
The traveller reached into his sack, 'It's twenty-four carat,' he claimed.

The keeper seized it and scrutinised it,
'It's not the correct one you twit,
Keep in mind at the crossroad, take a left and go round the bend,
At this rate your assignment will never end.'

Joshua Batt (11)
Wallington County Grammar School

The Midnight Call

I still remember that day,
Though it was long ago,
I still feel frightened and
Left not knowing what to say.

It happened on a summer's eve,
Oh, it wasn't very nice,
It had crept up to me quietly -
I could almost hear its breath.

A roar came from near by my back -
From that place behind me,
So I turned around to face it
And noticed that in courage, I lack.

I screamed in terror at what my eyes beheld,
It had a brown, square face,
With saliva rolling down its chin
And all around me, a poisonous gas I smelled.

So as quickly as I could, I fled,
Leaving it far behind,
But then, I thought, I can imagine quite well,
So I'll leave that monster in my head.

Anthony Hoskins (11)
Wallington County Grammar School

The Enchanted House

Clatter! Clatter! The sound of iron hooves hitting the
hard concrete ground,
The horse's eyes looking straight ahead.
Into what we could not see,
But what the bulky animal could.

Swish! Swish! The sound of the air singing in peace and harmony.
The houses lines up in one straight line,
With one in the middle standing out tall.
It made clear that it was king.

It stood for a second,
But then could not be seen.
Fascinating and interesting,
Bewitching and alluring.

It seemed an illusion,
But real to them.
They who lived
And never took rest.

Protection for their castle,
This could not be touched or harmed while they guarded,
Invisible they were,
But not to the eyes of the opposition.

They had arrived,
Sighs of relief,
was not complete,

Trapped

He rode off into the darkness of the forest
Upon a black horse, black as the night around him
Through the gaps in the trees he could faintly see the moon
It was full which didn't bother him much
All of a sudden he heard the sound of leaves being crushed
                                                    upon the floor
He thought it was just his horse although the sound was distant
He just kept galloping onwards, the sound kept getting *louder*
So he decided to keep moving in the direction of the sound
But the sounds were still just as distant as before
Suddenly he heard the sound of a river crashing upon the bank
He hadn't heard this sound that night
He travelled in search of the sound
He found nothing, abruptly the sound stopped, all was silent
He thought someone must be playing a trick on him
He gave a shout, 'It's not funny, stop it'
So he returned to the main path and rode onwards once more
All of a sudden he noticed something
Everything that went past was exactly the same as if he
                                                    wasn't even moving
So he changed direction and set off again
But the same thing occurred, everything that passed him
                                                    by was the same
Annoyed and angry he gave out a scream
'There's no way out of this place'
He rode off frantically in hot pursuit of an exit
His horse tired and hungry collapsed, so he continued on foot
He darted around, he thought maybe he was in a dream
But was he or was he trapped for an eternity in the forest?

Sean Farnsworth (11)
Wallington County Grammar School